FULLY *HALF* COMMITTED

*Conversation Starters
for Romantic Relationships*

BARBARA MORRISON & EDWARD RISLING

WOOD DRAGON BOOKS

Fully Half Committed:
Conversation Starters for Romantic Relationships
Copyright © 2019 by Barbara Morrison and Edward Risling
Inside and cover design: Callum Jagger

ISBN: 978-1-989078-16-7

Published by:
Wood Dragon Books
Post Office Box 429
Mossbank, Saskatchewan, Canada SOH 3G0
+1 306 591 7993

Cataloguing and Publications Data available from Library and Archives Canada.

To contact authors: See page 149

First Edition: September 2019

DEDICATION

With love,
we dedicate this book to our parents

Mary and Frank, married 62 years
Adeline and Joe, married 69 years

ACKNOWLEDGEMENTS

We gratefully acknowledge all the people who have walked through our doors, sat on our sofas in our respective offices, and began therapy with us. We feel privileged to have worked with people from all walks of life. We respect and admire the commitment of these individuals who were willing to do their own personal and relational work. Thank you!

We acknowledge and thank the presence of the hundreds of people who attended our *Fully Half Committed: Modern Day Relationships Conversation Cafes* in Saskatoon. Singles, couples, and people exploring open relationships were all a part of these evenings and their ages spanned across generations. We facilitated these free public groups for three years where we discussed all things related to relationships. Thank you!

We acknowledge our colleague, Scott Morrison, BA, BSW, MSW, RSW, who proposed the brilliant title of this book and the title of our workshops *(Fully Half Committed: Modern Day Relationships Conversation Cafe)*. Scott also co-facilitated several of the conversation groups. We appreciate and value his intelligence, humor, creativity, and kindness. He is a gifted second-generation therapist. Thank you!

We acknowledge our editor extraordinaire, Matthew Risling, BA, MA, Ph.D., for his patience while we struggled with words. Matthew also kept us focused as we had a tendency to get sidetracked. He was a magician at rewriting concepts we had written and is a master wordsmith. He also helped us with our dangling participles and misplaced modifiers. Thank you!

We acknowledge our publisher, Jeanne Martinson of Wood Dragon Books, whose encouragement helped to push us over the finish line. Her organization, ability to set deadlines, and directorial efforts were exactly what we needed to finish this book. Thank you!

We acknowledge all our beautiful children—Tanya, Matthew, Derek, Bridget, Kate and Scott—who are our cheerleaders. They encouraged us to complete this book and continue to remind us that we know what we are talking about. Thank you!

Like relationships, this book has been a labour of love. We want to acknowledge our spouses—Glenda and James—who have provided us with a demand for growth and who thought our idea for writing this book was a sound decision. Having said that, they will be happy that this book is complete!!

DISCLAIMER

When you are in an abusive relationship, you will be led to believe you are to blame for whatever form of abuse is perpetrated upon you. In fact, the hallmark of being on the receiving end of abuse is that you will start to believe that the abuse is justified.

No abuse is ever justified. Unless abusive behaviour is stopped, we do not recommend staying in a relationship where there is a presence of abuse of any type.

If you are in an abusive relationship where there is physical, sexual or emotional violence—or if you're in a relationship that is characterized by ridicule or fear of violence—we recommend you get in touch with your local crisis line and seek professional and legal support. Please visit these links for the following information on crisis lines within Canada and the U.S. and on warning signs of abuse:

Canada: http://endingviolencecanada.org/
www.canada.ca/en/public-health/topics/types-violence-abuse.html
The United States: www.thehotline.org

CONTENTS

NOTE
FROM THE AUTHORS

We are professional couples' therapists with a combined 60 years of experience who have worked with thousands of individuals and couples. In 1986, we met as students at the Faculty of Social Work in Saskatoon, Saskatchewan and in 2003 we became colleagues in private practice. We continue to have private practices offering individual, couples, and group therapy.

Our area of specialization is couples' therapy, which is a happy coincidence as we are both passionate about working with couples. We provide therapy for people in our city, province, country and throughout the world—in person and via distance therapy. We pride ourselves in offering intelligent and effective couples' therapy and collaborate on various projects related to relationships such as workshops, presentations, and facilitation of groups.

We consult with each other with the goal of providing the best possible therapy to our clients. Our approach to therapy is identical in that we adopt an anxiety-tolerance approach to therapy, as opposed to an anxiety-reduction approach. In other words, we work with our clients to assist them in taking care of their anxiety—*while* they work through personal and relationship issues with their partner. Tolerating anxiety is necessary for personal and relational growth.

The genesis of this book came about when we tossed out the idea of writing a book about the reoccurring themes we see in relationships. Offering bite-size chapters allows the reader to digest a complete idea within a small amount of information. We want our chapters to essentially be conversation starters for romantic relationships.

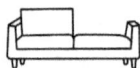

EDWARD RISLING

I consider myself to be an accidental therapist. I entered the profession because my wife at the time worked in mental health and I decided to follow in her footsteps. It was a fortunate accident as I discovered I had a passion and a talent for this work.

I was first married in 1972 and divorced about 20 years later. I remarried in 1998 to a woman I still love and live with. I am grateful to both women for the demands they placed on me to grow up—even though it was often a painful journey.

My real interest in doing relationship work was the result of the ending of my first marriage. The greatest gift my first wife gave me was to leave me. Her leaving gave me the opportunity to examine my marriage from a more distant vantage point. I realized that I had been in an accidental relationship, one where we had reacted to each other. We had lost sight of the big picture of our marriage. This was also a time when I began to realize that marriage (emotionally committed relationship) was an elegant, divinely inspired, people growing-up system.

Barbara and I became colleagues in 2003. As we shared our stories with each other, I would at times remark that I should write a book because I had knowledge to offer, but without any real intention of doing so. Barbara suggested that I should stop talking and start doing. Since I am coming to the end of my career, now is the time. She offered that she would be excited to co-author with me on this project and so a collaboration began.

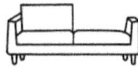

BARBARA MORRISON

My interest in reading biographies as an adolescent held a clue as to what career I would eventually pursue as an adult. I have a curiosity about people's lives, including their histories. When I was in my early 20s exploring options for a career, therapy and journalism were my two choices. There are always two-choice dilemmas in life. We bump into these choices many times and with every option we do not choose, there is a loss of what could have been. These losses are part of the human condition. For pragmatic reasons, I chose therapy. I'm so glad I did as I love the work I do.

For as long as I can remember, I have been interested in how relationships function. This curiosity led me to pursue a career specializing in couples' therapy. In 1984, I married my husband. Thirty-five years later, we continue to choose to share a life together.

The idea to write this book was first initiated by Ed, however ideas are only wishful thinking if we don't bring them to fruition. Ed tells me I was the one to insist we write this book and he is right. I became the taskmaster and Ed—a willing collaborator. The writing of this book has taken place on planes, trains, automobiles, offices, basements, and in various cities around the world. It has been a labour of love and tremendous fun.

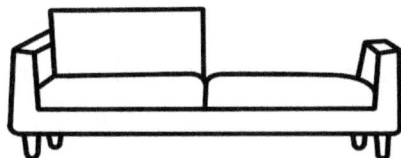

INTRODUCTION

BEING "FULLY HALF COMMITTED" is the elephant in the room in couples' therapy.

When it comes to romantic relationships, personal happiness now trumps relational longevity. People no longer view relationships as a commitment for life. The sentiment most often expressed by our clients is, "I will stay committed until I'm not happy anymore." The paradigm of long-term relationships has changed profoundly from one long-term commitment to one where a person now has two, three or more primary relationships over the course of their lifetime. This shift in thinking has resulted in a radical change in how we do therapy. We make no value judgment about the merit of staying single, or of having short-term or long-term relationships. What we do know is that people get together with passion, desire and energy for each other but eventually begin to react negatively to each other's stories.

Couples' therapy involves the therapist assisting the partners in working through developmental stages, differentiation and attachment issues, communication and negotiation skills, family-of-origin histories, assessments for psychological heath, sexual intimacy struggles, parenting differences and more. However, none of these strategies will matter if just one person is determined they want out. Every person who enters into a relationship has their own unique history, stories, and belief systems. These backgrounds bump into each other—either gently or with a sonic boom. Maintaining a relationship requires hard work and those in relationships may not always be happy; in fact, sometimes they will be downright miserable.

People who do not want to endure normal fluctuations in their relationship may choose to leave. For those who decide to weather the ups and downs in their relationship—this book is for you. It is for those who are curious about common struggles in relationships and seek advice for what to do when they are caught up in those struggles. This book is an invitation to become more conscious of how you function in a relationship. We hope it will benefit you in navigating the challenges of a partnership.

This book offers brief chapters of common struggles to get you thinking and engaged in conversation with others. Think of each chapter as a conversation starter.

You can open this book at any place and read a single chapter. You may want to have a conversation with your partner or share these ideas with friends or family. You may simply want to read our ideas for your own reflection.

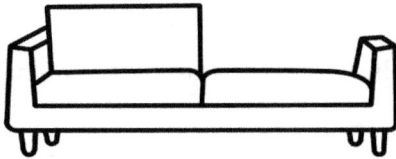

THE EVOLUTION OF FULLY HALF COMMITTED

A FEW YEARS AGO, Barbara had a client named Curtis who was perplexed by his unwillingness to fully commit to a relationship. He'd had a number of girlfriends over the years, some of whom he genuinely loved, but his relationships rarely lasted more than a year because he couldn't bring himself to make what he referred to as a "permanent commitment". When asked what a permanent commitment meant to him, he responded, "It's a promise to love someone unconditionally, for the rest of my life, and always put her needs ahead of mine." Curtis felt tremendous guilt for what he perceived as a selfish tendency to shrink from deep intimacy. "I do want a stable relationship," he insisted, "but how can I know I'll be happy with the same person ten years from now?"

While he felt himself to be abnormal, Curtis was articulating an experience that our clients have been expressing with ever more frequency. In recent years, we've noticed people becoming increasingly reticent to throw themselves into committed long-term relationships. It's not that they resist the idea of being part of a couple. To the contrary, most of our clients are all-in—but only up to a certain point. They are, as we say, *fully half-committed.*

Often people's willingness to commit terminates at distant, abstract periods in the future like "forever", or even, as Curtis said, "how will I know ten years from now my relationship will be intact?" Just as often, however, a relationship terminates when things stop being fun, when one or both partners stop feeling happy.

Does that willingness to end a relationship because it's no longer fun sound shallow to you? It doesn't to us. The fact is, the relationship landscape is undergoing a profound transformation. Relationships today simply don't have the same meaning or purpose as those of previous decades. Of course, there never was such a thing as a normal relationship, but there are broad cultural norms. And these have come up for negotiation. Rather than offering advice about what the new norms ought to be, this book is intended to help Curtis and those in his position become conscious in their own negotiations. Our purpose is to encourage readers to decide what they want from a relationship and to consider the work they need to do, and the sacrifices they need to make, in order to achieve their goal.

To best understand where our culture is today, it is useful to consider how we got here. The long-term monogamous relationship has been the standard model for generations. During that time, most people agreed that relationships were primarily procreative, sexually and emotionally exclusive, and were intended to last until death do us part. With no culturally sanctioned alternative, this tight interdependent structure encouraged people to become reliant on their partners for emotional validation. This structure also encouraged people to subordinate their desires first to the couple and later, it was presumed, to the family.

Today people are increasingly disinclined towards this traditional model. According to Statistics Canada (2016), the birth rate is as low as it has ever been, and the average age of new mothers is as high as it has ever been. Clearly, the reproductive unit is no longer the priority it once was. There is a growing emphasis on personal fulfillment, and a general sense that happiness is an individualistic endeavor. Many people now believe that accepting responsibility for other people's wellbeing may be an obstacle to their own.

So, why the shift? Why now? Of course, there's no simple answer to these questions, and we don't claim to be historians. There are, however, several factors we believe influenced the current paradigm. Perhaps the most obvious involves the wave of legal reforms that took place in the late 1960s, which introduced no-fault divorce, lowering barriers for men, and especially women, to end unhappy marriages. At around the same time, second-wave feminists began rallying for employment and income equality. Though there remains debate over the extent to which income equality has been achieved, there can be no doubt that women are much likelier to be financially independent now than they were in the past. This autonomy has allowed women to be choosier with their partners and freer to discontinue unsatisfying relationships.

But surely those factors alone can't account for Curtis's predicament or the recent trend towards fully half-committed relationships? As of 2016, the Canadian divorce rate (38%) was only slightly higher than it was in the mid-1990s (37%), and significantly lower than its peak in the mid-1980s (41%). That is to say, the availability of divorce doesn't correspond with changing relationship patterns. Neither does the trajectory of women's financial autonomy. While women's average income remains below men's, it has been rising steadily since the 1970s, with its most drastic upturn occurring at the turn of the 21st century. Why then is 2016 the first year on record when single Canadians above fifteen years of age outnumbered married ones? Why is the growth of short-term common-law unions outpacing the growth of marriages at a rate of five to one?

The answer has as much to do with popular culture as institutional and legal reform. The 1980s saw an explosion in the self-help industry. Publishers began churning out manuals for life, love, and happiness at a furious pace. At the same time, television personalities like Phil Donahue and Oprah Winfrey were pioneering an entertainment phenomenon. The syndicated talk show revolutionized media by turning its gaze away from glamorous musicians and movie stars to ordinary people with everyday issues.

Current cultural imperatives are having a radical influence on people's decisions to be in a relationship or not. Imperatives such as "I only live once", "Seize the day", "Make the most of out of life", "I have my own money so I don't need to have a partner", "I have lots of options and I'm going to exercise them", and "If I'm not happy with my partner, I'm not sticking around" are reflective of the current mindset. What were once secretive matters of personal and sexual discontent murmured in embarrassment to therapists and clergy, if spoken of at all, became matters of interest and entertainment.

We cannot overstate the impact of this phenomenom which has opened our personal lives to scrutiny and advice, in good ways and bad. The current change in relationship dynamics is spearheaded by a generation that grew up in a culture that emphasizes self-care, personal growth, and—above all—happiness.

Ironically, this happiness culture has created unique impediments to satisfying relationships. We have noted some common themes among our twenty- and thirty-something clients who report being discouraged at ever finding someone to share their lives with. First, there is a fear of settling for a relationship that is less than perfect. TV and movies celebrate the act of falling in love, but rarely address the work involved with staying in love. Secondly, there is an ever-greater availability of possible matches through online dating and dating apps. Thus, young people are strongly encouraged to remain dissatisfied, and to keep at least one eye open for a more suitable partner.

People often say they want to "work on themselves" before they fully commit to someone. They may date for a while and then leave that relationship to do their personal work. The problem with this strategy is that people always have their own personal work to do and that means they will never fully commit.

Since happiness is now a high cultural priority, it makes sense that many people would engage in multiple relationships that bring short-term excitement at a minimal emotional cost, rather than long-term commitments that require constant upkeep after the romantic sheen has worn off. This is a perfectly reasonable approach to dating, and if those are the sort of relationships that make you happy, then you may not need this book. If you're more like Curtis, however, and you're struggling to achieve both personal fulfillment and a committed relationship, then this book offers encouragement and advice about how to do so.

It is possible to have a fulfilling personal life and a meaningful romantic relationship. Additionally, learning to acknowledge your own priorities as an individual within a unit makes you more able to understand your partner's priorities as well. Deciding what you both want from a relationship and communicating that to each other gives you the best chance of achieving your goals and precludes many of the insecurities and tensions that come from having to guess. Maintaining a fully committed relationship requires constant effort from both parties, but is effort well spent which can pay huge dividends in happiness and emotional security.

1

ACCEPT "NO"

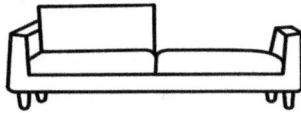

ASKING FOR CHANGE IN A RELATIONSHIP is unavoidable. We encounter behaviours or characteristics in our partner that irritate or upset us. We want more of the good stuff, like cooperation with housework and affection—and we want less of the bad stuff, like moodiness and excuses.

Often our partners are willing to accommodate us, or at least compromise, but occasionally they are not. The "not" may be for several reasons, such as "This is who I am," or "I want to do it my way." But no matter the reason or how it is expressed, we must learn to accept when our requests have been refused.

When your partner refuses to change their behaviour, it is up to you to choose how to proceed. Will you accept it as an unfortunate fact of life that your partner rarely does dishes or picks up their socks, or will you start looking for someone more considerate? Either option may be reasonable (as long as you call things off before you start looking elsewhere). What is not reasonable, however, is ceaseless nagging about a matter that really isn't up for discussion.

John and Mary have been married for eight years. John is a recovering alcoholic. He is heavily involved in AA and insists Mary be involved too. She attends the occasional Al Anon meeting but continues to drink socially. John regularly asks Mary to quit drinking, but she still likes to go out with her sisters from time to time and come home with a soft glow. John believes Mary's drinking is a threat to his sobriety, but he clings to the hope that he may convince her to change her "selfish" behaviour. What John needs to accept, however, is that Mary has already given her answer, and it's not his place to keep pushing. Instead, he owes it to both of them to figure out a way to live with her decision or leave the relationship.

What habits or behaviours has your partner asked you to change that you are unwilling to change?

What habits or behaviours have you asked your partner to change that they are unwilling to change?

2

ACCEPT THAT NOTHING IS FOREVER

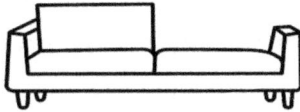

EVERYTHING COMES TO AN END, even us. Either you or your partner will experience the pain inherent when one of you leaves the relationship. This may be the result of a decision by either of you that you no longer want to be with the other or it may be through the death of one or the other. The only possible exception to this is the rare occurrence in which you die together.

Having this awareness, and loving anyway, is an act of courage. Saying to your partner, "You have my permission to go first. I will carry on if you're the one to leave first," is an act of love. This is a statement that reflects confidence in your own resilience and in your ability to survive the loss. This is true whether the leaving is through death by disease, accident, or old age. By staying aware of the transience of your existence, you can maintain a perspective on your conflicts and keep the big picture of your relationship in mind.

Be aware throughout the course of your day about the concept of impermanence.
In doing so, see what impact this has on you.
Develop a plan of what you will do if your partner leaves before you.
Imagine if this was the last day or week you would have with your partner.

3

ACCEPT THAT YOU WILL HURT EACH OTHER

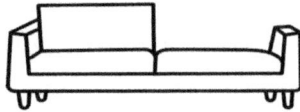

MANY OF US HAVE A FANTASY. We want to believe that we can have a relationship in which we are loved unconditionally, understood completely and accepted without reservation. Not only is this impossible, it would interfere with the growth demanded of us by our marriage.

Being hurt and feeling pain are part of the human condition and are experienced by the most loving and committed of couples. By understanding and accepting that you are going to experience pain in your relationship, you can put your energy into building tolerance and strengthening yourself rather than becoming resentful of your partner's shortcomings. You also need to accept that you are as messed up as your partner and that you are the cause of some of their pain.

The next consideration is one of how to make repair when you are hurt or when you hurt the other. Person A (the offender) has the responsibility to make a move to repair. Person B has the responsibility to allow that repair to take place or to communicate what is necessary from person A in order for the repair to happen.

Tyler and Telia have a niece who lives in the same community.

Telia: *Ashley went out of town for the weekend and asked if we would be willing to check in on and feed and water her cats. I said we would. Would you like to come with me and do that now?*

Tyler: *Sure, it's a nice day, let's take my scooter.*

Once at the house, Telia suggested: *Let's stay for a while and be company for the cats. We can play a game of Scrabble while we're here.*

Tyler agreed and they commenced to play. As the game progressed, Tyler realized that he was being soundly beaten. Telia was a hundred points ahead and there were only 12 tiles left.

Tyler: *I concede, there is no way I will be able to catch up to you.*

Telia: *Oh, so you're just going to give up? I didn't think I married a quitter.*

Intending to be playful, Telia also had a 7 letter, 62-point word she wanted to play. Tyler was hurt and offended and responded with anger.

Tyler: *That is a demeaning and shaming comment and I am done playing with you.*

They leave the house both feeling hurt and get on the scooter to return home.

Several blocks into the ride, Telia poked Tyler in the ribs. Tyler understood that she had made a move to repair but, being the offended party, he shoved his elbow back and refused the repair. Another few blocks, at the top of a bridge, at a red light, she again poked him in the ribs and he again refused the repair.

Telia: *Tyler, I am trying to make repair. Are you going to let it in?*

Having been confronted in such a clear and direct manner and knowing that if he rejected the repair, she would not likely make another attempt, at least not for a long time, Tyler relented.

Tyler: *I will let it in at the bottom of the bridge.*

With that statement, he allowed the repair to take place.

How do you hold onto resentment?
How do you withhold repair?
How do you harm your partner through words or actions?
How can you make a repair sooner than later?

4

BALANCE CONNECTION AND AUTONOMY

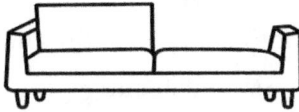

BALANCING CONNECTION WITH ANOTHER, while maintaining autonomous functioning (expressing your thoughts opinions, feelings, desires, wants, behaviours) is called differentiation. In the context of relationships, differentiation means that both people are developing a Self in the relationship. Stated another way, differentiation is the balance between a connection with another and personal autonomy—both exist simultaneously.

Often people think they need to be "on the same page" with the other when making decisions or even when having an opinion about something. Clearly, this is not always possible. When one person coerces the other into thinking or feeling the way they do, this is called fusion. When fusion occurs, one person loses who they are.

Every day, couples are required to make decisions. These decisions are both minor and major. For example, you might agree to having a joint bank account for all household expenses (connection) but also have independent and separate checking accounts for personal expenses (autonomy). For those in a blended family, you may decide to parent your own children, but not your stepchildren, thus having your own autonomy to make decisions about parenting decisions. Elements necessary for healthy differentiation are a willingness to not only listen to each other's opinions and feelings, but also a willingness to compromise and negotiate.

Compromise and negotiation can mean different things. An example of a compromise would be when two parents want different curfew times for their adolescent. One parent is fine with 2 a.m. as the curfew and the other parent wants an 11:30 p.m. curfew. They end up compromising on a 12:30 a.m. curfew.

Negotiation, on the other hand, can result in one person getting what they want and the other not getting what they want. These are situations where compromises cannot be made. For example, if one person does not believe in spanking a child and the other does, an unlikely compromise would be to "lightly" spank a child. A negotiation process would therefore involve each person trying to influence the other person by arguing the merits of their opinion about discipline. When one person decides to go along with the other person's way of disciplining, that person will either accept their loss graciously or will be resentful.

Compromise and negotiation are inherent throughout a relationship, every day, in small and big decisions. Couples can reach a resolution by working through decisions. Then they must both decide if they can live with the outcome of that decision without resentment.

Barbara worked with a couple facing differentiation.

Susie: *We've come to talk to you because we are having the same fight all the time and we don't know how to resolve this. We just keep going around in circles and getting nowhere.*

Barbara: *Tell me what's happening.*

Susie: *I think it's really important that we take the kids to church every Sunday and Michael doesn't like to go to church. When I ask him to go, he says "no" and he stays at home and does whatever he wants.*

Barbara: *Do you go to church, Susie, and do the kids go?*

Susie: *Yes, we do, but I think it's important that we all go, including Michael. It's important for the kids that we are all together in going to church. What does it say to them when their dad stays home and just I take them? This is confusing to them.*

Michael: *I'm not stopping you or the kids from going to church and I'm not asking you to stay home either. If you think it's confusing for them, just stay home, don't go to church and it won't be confusing for them.*

Susie: *That's his answer all the time.*

Michael: *I won't be going to church. I'm an atheist. As I've said before, she can take the kids and go because it's important to her and I'm okay with the kids going.*

Susie: *This is just wrong. This will mess up the kids.*

Barbara: *Let me offer you a perspective. You won't have the same thoughts, opinions and desires as each other all the time. That is a given. Your children won't be messed up unless you make this a problem. In fact, your children will have respect for each of you when you support each other's interests and beliefs. It will only be a problem if you criticize or denigrate the other parent's thoughts and feelings about an issue. In this case, Susie, you want to go to church and you want to take the children. So, do that. Michael is supporting your decision. Michael, you don't want to go to church, so don't. When Susie and the children come home from church, invest time in asking them about their experience at church that morning. Show an interest and support Susie's choice to go with the kids.*

Susie: *But what will happen when the kids are older, like teenagers, and decide they don't want to go because their dad doesn't go?*

Barbara: *You will have to decide at that point whether it is important to you that the children at that age have their own autonomy to make their choices, even if those choices are different from yours. This will be a parenting decision on your part—let your children decide at that point or you will decide that they have to go and indicate as much to them.*

In this example, differentiation is evident in the following ways: Susie and Michael are adults and they each decide what they want to do and support each other's decision (autonomy + connection).

Is there room in your relationship for more than one opinion, one way of doing something, one way of feeling? Or do you find yourself thinking that you have to be "on the same page"?
What does too much autonomy lead to?
What does too much connection lead to?

5

BE AWARE OF DEATH BY PECKING

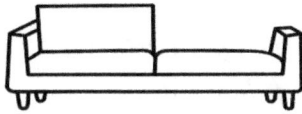

IT'S NOT UNUSUAL FOR PEOPLE to peck away at their partner. Pecking, in this context, means taking pot shots, being sarcastic, mean, cruel—slowly and insidiously chipping away at the psyche of someone they say they love. These are domestic terrorist tactics people use in their relationships, as if they are at war. We consider this to be "death by pecking."

There are many reasons people do this. If you are the pecker, you may want to self-confront and gain insight as to why you do this. Decide if you want to continue being emotionally abusive to your partner. If you wish to improve your behaviour, think about your tendency to peck and stop yourself before you speak or do something that brings harm to your partner.

If you are the peckee and are turning a blind eye to your partner's behaviour, your partner will lose respect for you and continue to treat you poorly. He doesn't have to self-confront because you essentially collude in this dance of contempt. If you don't want to turn a blind eye to this emotional manipulation, you must be accountable to speak up and confront your partner. Either their behaviour will change or not. Relationships that are characterized by constant pecking will end in the death of a thousand cuts.

Consider seeing a therapist if you are in a relationship where confrontation has resulted in abuse.

6

BE CURIOUS ABOUT YOUR PARTNER

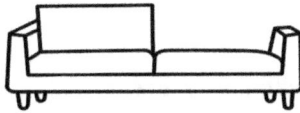

PEOPLE IN RELATIONSHIPS tend to think they know everything there is to know about their partner. They can even be a bit smug about it. Being too confident in a fixed idea of who your partner is and isn't can lead to complacency and boredom. No matter how long you've been together, or how comfortable you both are in your lives, it is important to invest energy into learning more about your partner. If you remain curious about your partner, they may continue to surprise you.

Kyla and Yumi have been together twelve years. At one point, they recognized they had become prone to taking each other for granted. They wanted to re-engage their curiosity about the other, so they started coming up with games to help rekindle the mystery that first attracted them.

On Kyla's birthday, Yumi gave her a card with two $100 bills enclosed—one for each of them. The card instructed them to use the $100 to plan and complete an activity they had never done before. Their activities would be separate. Kyla and Yumi wouldn't tell the other what they were doing until afterwards when they met up at a wine bar. They would take turns sharing their new experience and the listener wouldn't interrupt except to ask questions. Through this conversation, Kyla and Yumi each learned new things about the other.

There are endless ways to cultivate curiosity in a relationship and they don't need to be expensive. We've heard interesting accounts from clients about how they've taken our advice to re-discover each other. They've planned elaborate treasure hunts, playful questionnaires, and day trips to nearby places that neither had been to before.

The point is, once you decide to spend the energy, it's a lot of fun to arouse and sustain curiosity about your partner—which makes for a happier, more successful relationship.

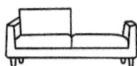

If you're in a relationship, imagine some ideas that you can initiate to learn more about your partner. Here's one to get you started: Ask your partner about a pivotal moment in their life.

7

BE DILIGENT WITH PERSONAL HABITS

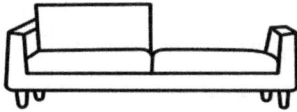

OVER TIME, IF RELATIONSHIPS BECOME ROUTINE, couples become less considerate of each other, and sex starts to drop off. If you find yourself in this situation and you want to reverse it or if you're not there yet and you don't want to be, then you must make sure to put in the effort. Your return is likely to be commensurate with the energy invested.

If you're the type who can be indifferent to laundry and showers, and you notice your sex life has become a bit sluggish, you may want to connect the dots. Wash regularly and wear clean clothes. Personal hygiene goes a long way towards making yourself the kind of person your partner wants to connect with intimately.

For some, this directive can be difficult to express. It is much more pleasant to kiss someone who has clean teeth. Our clients sometimes tell us they don't want to embarrass their partners by bringing up the topic of stinky breath. Yet, failing to disclose such matters means choosing low sexual desire over an awkward conversation.

We advise against failing to disclose, especially since sexual disconnection is one of the top relationship killers. It's okay to tell your partner to up their hygiene game, so long as you do it with care. Be courageous and let your partner know that you would love to connect with them once they've brushed their teeth or showered. Creating a healthy and robust relationship requires that you respect your partner enough to be honest with them.

If you're in a relationship and are withholding information from your partner, write down your complaints. Decide whether you will give the list to your partner or tell them in person.

8

BE HONEST

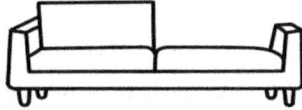

THIS SOUNDS LIKE COMMON SENSE GUIDANCE, but being honest with yourself and with your partner is not always easy. Lack of honesty shows up in lying by commission or lying by omission. There are many reasons why people choose to overtly lie and why people choose not to reveal their thoughts and feelings. Whether the lying is by omission or commission, problems will ensue that will catapult the couple into distress or crisis.

In our therapy practices, we subscribe to an anxiety-tolerance approach to relationships, rather than an anxiety-reduction approach. The difference? In an anxiety-reduction approach to relationships, in order to reduce anxiety for themselves or for their partner, a person will not be honest. In an *anxiety-tolerance* approach to relationships, a person will be truthful regardless of the anxiety the truth may cause themself or their partner. This approach takes courage and an ability to manage anxiety. When a person communicates what might be difficult for their partner to hear, it sends a message that their partner is respected enough to be told the truth—even if it's difficult to hear. Their partner may struggle with whatever is being conveyed, but that struggle is necessary. In fact, it's essential for the relationship to grow.

In an *anxiety-reduction* approach to relationships, a person will not be honest, either by omission or commission, in order to spare themself or their partner the anxiety that their disclosure may cause. When the anxiety reduction approach is used, resentments will build, unhappiness will ensue, depression will be felt, betrayals may occur, and disillusionment will set in. This will be a recipe for disaster.

For those of you in therapy, make note of whether your therapist works from an *anxiety-tolerance* or an *anxiety-reduction* approach to therapy itself. Therein lies the difference between receiving effective therapy and not-so-effective therapy. If your therapist is not fully honest, how can their therapy be truly effective?

Regardless of whether you are in relationship with a romantic partner, friend, sibling, or colleague—be aware of when you want to disclose something that is important to you, but that may be difficult for someone to hear. Then say this to yourself and jump in: "What I have to say is important to me and it may be hard for _____ to hear. I am going to muster up the courage to say it anyway in a manner that is assertive, not aggressive or passive. If _____ is upset with what I have said, I will remember that they will have whatever experience they will have and that their struggle is necessary in order for our relationship to grow. I will respect myself and _____ by being honest and truthful. After that, it's out of my hands. I will be accountable to myself and to the relationship."

9

BE IMAGINATIVE

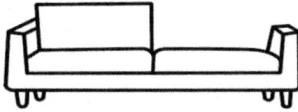

WHEN YOU STRETCH YOUR CREATIVE MIND, you have an opportunity to live a richer, more meaningful existence. Exercising your creativity combats boredom. You are more interesting, not only to yourself but also to your partner, if you use your imagination—whether that to be to solve new problems, to make art, to think of new activities, or to engage in new experiences.

Albert Einstein offered this about imagination: "Imagination is more important than knowledge. For knowledge is limited, whereas imagination embraces the entire world, stimulating progress, giving birth to evolution."

Imagination ignites passion and is a creative avenue to experience joy and adventure.

If you think of an idea that you can surprise your partner with, you show that you have spent time thinking about that person. These acts of imagination and creativity go a long way in making your partner feeling loved. Loving consciously requires imagination, time, energy, and commitment.

Using your imagination, write down ideas to enhance your relationship and your own life.
What new activities would you and your partner be willing to commit to?

10

BE MORE INTENTIONAL

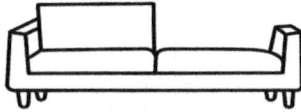

IF YOU WANT TO CREATE A HEALTHY RELATIONSHIP, you must be willing to move beyond intention. It is not enough to just *intend* to be loving, kind, imaginative, loyal, or honest. You must actually *be* loving, kind, imaginative, loyal, and honest. It is not enough to intend to be thoughtful or considerate. You must behave in thoughtful and considerate ways.

It is not enough to intend to make a change. If a change has been found to be necessary, you must make the change. It is not enough to want to be a better person or partner, you must become what you say you want to be.

People change for three main reasons.

1. Because of a crisis.
2. Because of a growing sense of dis-ease or distress
    that culminates in an experience of disgust.
3. Because they discover it is possible for them to change.

This is not to suggest that change is easy, for it is not. Only that it is possible and that if one has committed to change, there is no good excuse not to follow through.

What changes have you made due to crisis, dis-ease, distress, or disgust?
What changes have you made because you suddenly realized that change was possible?
What are some new changes you would like to make?

11

CHOOSE YOUR RESPONSE

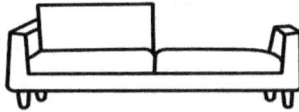

IF YOU WANT AN INTENTIONAL RELATIONSHIP, you must be conscious about what you want out of it. This does not mean putting your own needs before your partner's. To the contrary, it is imperative that you both articulate your expectations and desires to yourself and to each other. When you are clear about this, you can interpret and respond to each other in a way that is consistent with the kind of relationship you intend to create.

Meet Andy and Cass, married nine years. They are enjoying an evening out with several new couple friends. Andy is a gregarious and entertaining storyteller, and he is telling the one about ... Cass grabs his knee and says, "You're not telling it right." She then proceeds to complete the narrative in a way that makes her look like a patient, long-suffering wife and makes Andy look like something of an ass … or at least that's how he takes it. Andy is startled at first and then offended. He gets a small hit of adrenaline. He doesn't want to seem like a bad sport in front of his new friends, but he envisions having words with her on the drive home.

Andy then notices Cass's energy as she completes her story. She is animated and excited, and he's unsure how to understand this energy. Is she deliberately trying to embarrass him, maybe even punish him for something? Does she feel like it's her turn for the spotlight, or does she just really like this story? It occurs to him that the significance of Cass's conduct and his reaction to her version of the story is more dependent on his internal narrative than on her behaviour and he realizes that he has a choice to make. He can decide to take her interruption as a gesture of disrespect, or he can take it as an unintentional slight from an assertive woman whose vibrant energy has always attracted him. The drive home will be very different depending on which reality he opts to accept and upon which traits he chooses to focus. He asks himself the crucial question, "What kind of relationship do I want to create?" Put in these terms, his next step becomes obvious, and he and Cass continue to enjoy their evening out.

In our years of working as couple therapists, a common, contentious and utterly useless argument is the one about who gets to define reality. We often ascribe intentions to our partner that are completely off-base and we use our emotional reactions as evidence for our version of events.

It's useful to know that there is no such thing as reality. Reality is mostly a fluid construct that depends upon our own experience and state of mind. Once we are aware of this, we become free to scrutinize our own interpretation of things and are more likely to assume a generous attitude.

Ask yourself at least once a day:

1. *"What is my attitude towards my partner?"*
2. *"Is this consistent with the kind of marriage I want and am working to create?"*

If the answer to question #2 is "no" – change your attitude or deal with the conflict that is triggering this attitude.

12

COMMIT TO A YEARLY CHECKUP

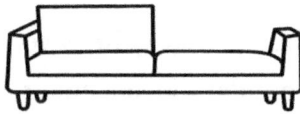

PHYSICIANS ADVISE A YEARLY CHECK-UP to maintain health and ensure minor ailments do not become major illnesses. We believe the same strategy should apply to relationships. Couples frequently enter therapy as a last resort when the relationship has become untenable—or nearly so. While it's often possible to pull back from the brink of disaster, it's far easier to work on relationships that haven't started to teeter yet. One or two sessions a year with a couples' therapist can go a long way towards maintaining harmony and preventing crises.

If intervention is left too late, partners may become ambivalent about their desire to be in the relationship and their energy to invest in working through their difficulties may be limited at best. This is not to say that therapy can't help at this point—it's just more difficult. Clients regularly tell us, "We waited so long that even if our marriage could be made better, I don't have any feelings left for my partner and I can't imagine those feelings coming back."

When couples get married, they do not necessarily know what their struggles will be or how they will handle adversity. No one knows exactly how they will handle exes, in-laws, job stress, parenting differences, religious differences, illness, mental health issues, blended families, domestic division of labor, finances, or sex. Couples often see problems as a sign that their relationship is in trouble. If addressed early, however, such challenges can actually strengthen bonds and encourage communication and emotional growth.

When did you last search out professional help for your relationship? When was the last time you had a chat with your partner about how you deal with the potential struggles inherent in a love relationship?

13

COMMUNICATE WITH INTENT

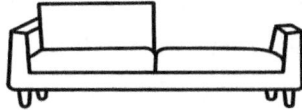

THE REASON WE COMMUNICATE is that we have an intention and are looking for a particular outcome (effect). One of the principles of a successful relationship is that couples pay attention to the "intention" of each other.

Many of us attempt to communicate our intention through the use of telepathy—a means of communication that is rarely successful! However, it is interesting and helpful to note that the *internal* experience of the person using telepathy is the sense that they have actually communicated their intention. The words we use are often interpreted differently by the receiver of the message than was intended by the sender.

Jennifer tells her husband, "I want you to be more considerate of me." He agrees and works harder at acknowledging the contributions she makes to running the household. Jennifer is still dissatisfied because what she really wants is for him to have more patience for the time it takes her to get ready for work. This example illustrates a simple misunderstanding based on the individuals' differing understanding of the word *considerate*.

Words are only one part of the communication process. Communication also includes our tone of voice, the expression on our face, the orientation of our body, the interpretations of behaviour, context, and when and where we are during the interaction.

Dave and Sally have been married six years and are still very much in love. Sally makes an appointment with a therapist and comes in alone for the first session. She also made an appointment for her husband and then one for them together.

In Sally's private session: *I really love my husband. He is a great man, a wonderful father and a hard worker. The problem is that my husband wants sex every day. I like having sex with him, but this is more than I want. I don't want to hurt his feelings and I'm not sure how to approach him about this.*

Dave comes in for his private appointment the following week.

Dave: *I'm not sure why I am coming. My marriage is pretty good. I really love my wife. She is an exceptional woman, and a terrific mother. I guess if there is an issue for me, it would be that she wants sex every day. I do like sex with her but every day is a little more than I want. I've not discussed this with her because I don't want to hurt her feelings.*

Sally and Dave attended the third session together.

Therapist: *So, tell me how do you let each other know you are interested in making love?*

Sally: *Well my husband gets up every morning, shaves, showers and puts on cologne and then goes to work. When he comes home, we have family time until we put the kids to bed. Then he goes upstairs, has another shower, shaves, puts on cologne and I know he wants to make love. So, I respond.*

Dave (mouth hanging open): *Actually, I just have a really heavy beard. If I don't shave again at night, it scratches and drives me crazy and I shave in the shower, so I don't leave little hairs in the sink.*

Sally: *Oh my God.*

This amusing example shows how even the most loving of couples may misinterpret the behaviours or signals sent by the other.

Be aware of the intention of what you want to communicate as it will contribute to the outcome of the conversation. What exactly do you want from the conversation?
Practice asking your partner what they desire to achieve in a conversation.

14

CONTRACT FOR A YEAR AT A TIME

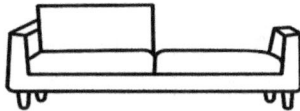

IMAGINE IF YOU CHECK IN WITH YOUR PARTNER every twelve months to see if you want to sign on for another year?

Here are some suggestions for conversation starters:

1. How is this relationship working for you?
2. What are the things about me that you value and appreciate?
3. What are the things about me that you might want changed?
4. What are the things about our relationship that you love?
5. What are areas of our relationship that you think we can work on?

6. What is something beneficial that you offer to the relationship?
7. What is something you do that is harmful to our relationship or to me that you will work on changing?
8. What is something that I bring to the relationship that is of value?
9. What is something I do that has been harmful to you or our relationship that I could change?

When the above are posed and answered from a place of curiosity and compassion, you are nurturing and taking care of your relationship. You can use these questions and others of your own to inquire about each other's experiences.

Consider seeking couples' therapy twice a year—or at the very least, once per year. If you want to have a long-term relationship with your partner, this is the surest way of preventing relationship challenges going from a minor issue to a larger one. Seeing a therapist also allows you to pause and have a conversation about what is working well between the two of you.

Set a time to complete your questions and have your partner do the same. Then discuss.

15

CONTRIBUTE TO EACH OTHER'S HAPPINESS

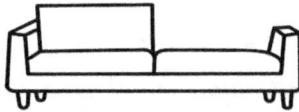

CONTRARY TO THE CURRENT CULTURAL IMPERATIVE of "It's not up to me to make you happy", we believe that the satisfaction people feel in a relationship is determined in large part due to each person contributing to the other's happiness. This, of course, is true in relationships of all kinds—friends, siblings, parents and children, and work colleagues.

There is a great deal of emphasis on self care in today's western society. However, we propose the idea of *"we care"*, which implies the importance of taking care of each other in mutually beneficial ways. In order to ensure an optimal level of relationship satisfaction, it is important to remember that two people have *chosen* each other in order to create a life together. It is up to the two people to ensure their own happiness as well as the happiness of the other. In order to contribute to the joy your partner feels, you need to be curious as to what will bring joy to that person. Paying attention to what your partner is interested in, what makes them smile, what promotes contentment, and what makes your partner feel most alive will give clues into what you can do to contribute to their happiness.

Whether you are in a romantic relationship or in a relationship with a friend, sibling, parent, child, or colleague, think of what you can do to contribute to the other person's happiness and joy and go do it.

16

CREATE ALIVENESS

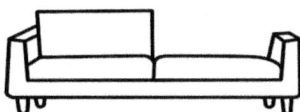

OUR BODIES WANT TO OPERATE in the most efficient manner possible. This translates into predictable patterns. We also develop habitual ways of interacting with each other and can become lazy and predictable. Sex is often the first casualty of relationships that have lost their aliveness. Intimacy becomes infrequent and perfunctory. But as our clients tell us again and again, what they miss most is the excitement of being together.

Being alive in life and in relationship doesn't just happen. If you want a fun and passionate relationship, you must create fun and passion.

Jason and Luanne have been in a committed relationship for 15 years. This is a second marriage for each of them and they're determined not to make the same mistakes they made the first time around. They are experiencing a loss of energy and excitement that characterized their early years. Luanne decided that she wasn't happy with the state of affairs and made an appointment with the therapist.

Luanne: *I really love my husband and I don't want to leave him, but things feel so predictable and boring that I am feeling numb. I don't know what to do.*

Therapist: *Have you talked with Jason about this and communicated how dissatisfied you are with the status quo?*

Luanne: *Well I've tried and he gets all defensive and we just end up having a fight. I've become so discouraged I don't even try anymore.*

Therapist: *Do you know what you want? What are the changes you would like to see?*

Luanne: *Well I would like him to be more spontaneous and more playful. I'd like him to spend more time with me and I would like to do more things together.*

Therapist: *How willing are you to do the work you need to do to get what you want?*

Luanne: *I'll do whatever it takes.*

Therapist: *Since Jason's not here, I'm going to suggest that, instead of complaining about what you're not getting in the relationship, you try experimenting with creating what you want. For example, if you want more spontaneity or playfulness, decide to be more playful and spontaneous yourself. You want more aliveness, so see what happens when you become more alive. Jason may respond the way you would like him to, and he may not. You may experience rejection and you'll have to deal with that. Or you may find that he responds positively, and you get to enjoy that. Either way, you're being active and responsible in creating the aliveness that you want. I promise that this is a lot healthier than waiting for it to come from him.*

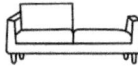

Take turns, each week, planning a social event or activity. Get out your calendars and mark the date and time that this will happen. Do things you've never done before.

17

CREATE THE RELATIONSHIP YOU WANT

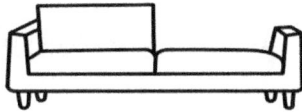

MOST PEOPLE WHO GET MARRIED WANT TO HAVE, and believe they have, an extra-ordinary connection with each other. Furthermore, they expect that this connection is strong enough to sustain without a great deal of effort. Every couple starts out with a big barrel of mutual goodwill and as long as the barrel is topped up, they default to a positive response and/or repair easily the misunderstandings and conflicts that all marriages experience.

However, what is more common is that partners become lazy over time and don't do the daily maintenance that a good marriage requires. Their barrel of goodwill starts to empty. When this happens, they start reacting to one another, then reacting to the reactions—until after several years, they look over at each other and wonder, "How did we get here?"

To increase your odds of having a better than average relationship, you must be deliberate. Be clear about what you want in your relationship and then act in a conscious way, every day, to create it. If you want your spouse to default in a positive way towards you, you must behave in a way that encourages that reaction. For example, you can perform an on-purpose act of kindness towards your partner every day. If you want play to be a part of your marriage, you need to be playful every day. This can be in how you engage with each other sexually, participate in activities you enjoy together, share projects, or in respectful teasing.

On a cold February evening, Dallas and Delaney had just attended a family wedding and were walking the block and a half back to their hotel room. It was -40 C and the hotel had an outside entrance.

Delaney: *Dallas, hurry open the door. I'm freezing!*

Dallas: *Here, hold this.*

Dallas hands Delaney a frozen dog bone he had picked up, while he fumbles with the door. She holds the bone for several seconds and then she realizes what she has in her hand. She laughs and tosses it back at him affectionately.

Delaney: *You are such a shit.*

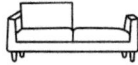

With intention and deliberateness, at the end of each day, tell each other what worked well between the two of you that day.

18

CULTIVATE AWARENESS

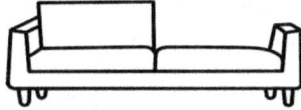

A WOMAN WAS IN THERAPY to try and salvage a marriage in which she still loved her partner. The relationship was falling apart because of neglect. Whenever she attempted to communicate her despair to her partner, he would deny his neglect or deflect back blame. She was loved by a partner who was unwilling to seriously consider the part he played in her unhappiness. He was fine with how their relationship was and if she was unhappy "she" should do something about it.

During her therapy session, she said, "Even though I try to make myself aware, I realize that I've missed and misinterpreted a great deal. If people who are making a conscious effort to be aware of what's going on miss so much, what's happening to those who are in a state of unawareness? Are they even aware that there is a possibility that they are misinterpreting?"

We have been asked this question, or a variation of it, many times and there are several reasons why people stay unaware. Some people are relationship lazy and don't want to do the work it takes to make a change. They are invested in having their partner do the relational work, actively resisting any attempt from their partner to push them to engage in self-exploration. Some people will be defensive and perceive a request for self-exploration as a criticism or an indication of not being good enough and will therefore avoid the uncomfortable feelings that come with self-confrontation. The anxiety of being self-aware is intolerable to some people and they will avoid it at all costs, even if it means losing the relationship.

Some humans are psychologically minded more than others and find it much easier and interesting to be introspective and self-aware. Others lack the ability to be introspective and examine *Self* in this way. To be aware requires a level of abstraction, the ability to step outside of *Self* and observe *Self* as object, not just experience *Self* as subject. These people will be aware of the impact others have on them but are unaware of the impact they have on others. They will be confused and reactive and feel "in over their heads" when dealing with interpersonal issues. They will then resort to defence mechanisms such as denial, anger, blame, projection, and deflection—or a combination of these.

Becoming self-aware can be painful. Self-confronting and becoming aware of your harmful behaviours inevitably leads to feelings of shame. Confronting your shame requires fortitude and courage along with the ability to self-soothe. Once you become self-aware, you can no longer lie to yourself about the impact you've had on your partner or the responsibility you have to repair.

Even though we hear people say they want to grow, many people pay lip service to these ideas and aren't prepared to do the work. What we have just described is the work. This is personal and relational growth. The reward of living a conscious life is worth it.

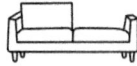

When was I last challenged by another regarding my behaviour? How did I react?

19

CULTIVATE EROTIC TENSION

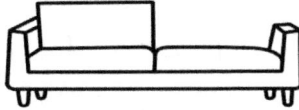

SOME PEOPLE KEEP THE EXCITEMENT AND MYSTERY going by engaging in alternative relationships such as open and polyamorous relationships or swinging. This chapter is written for those people who choose a monogamous relationship.

Maintaining erotic tension with the same someone over a period of years requires both partners being active and intentional. Most partners want sexual tension yet don't always achieve it. Many people stop feeling sexual desire for their partner, resulting in the relationship suffering from neglect.

As David Deida states in his book, *The Way of the Superior Man*, "Because you expect your intimate relationship to serve so many purposes it begins to veer towards the utilitarian. By constantly talking to your partner about finances, work, household and children, you turn your partner into a neutral companion. You become so familiar with each other that the mystery of sexual enchantment becomes standardized into the ritual mechanics of kiss, stroke, lick, pump and snore."

If, however you want to keep eroticism alive within the context of a monogamous relationship, you must be willing to do the work and play required—this is what is meant by a labor of love. Nurturing a friendship requires that you give it time, presence, interest, and effort. You need to be aware of your attitude toward your partner and take responsibility for maintaining a positive one. To keep erotic tension requires the same kind of energy, awareness, insight, and effort.

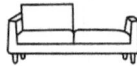

How do I turn myself on?
What is it about me that I find exciting? (This may include fantasy, how I dress, or what planning I might do prior to a sexual encounter.)
How do I keep myself from getting excited or feeling desire?
What turns me on about my partner?
What turns me off about my partner?
What would I be willing to consider?
What would my partner be willing to consider?
Enter into a discussion with your partner, with these questions as a starting point.

20

CULTIVATE INTIMACY
IN DAILY LIFE

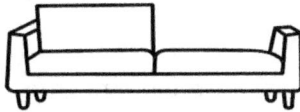

IT'S A RARE PERSON who enters our office and does not say that they are stressed and overwhelmed in life. When asking them about their typical day, we hear that there are three jobs involved—paid work, volunteer work, and the non-paid work of domestic maintenance of a home and parenting (for those people who have children). In addition to these three jobs, there is an attempt to stay in physical shape, engage in social activities with family and friends, attend medical appointments, travel, spend time in nature, and so on.

The bar has been raised on humans' stress levels. So high, in fact, many people are experiencing increased levels of anxiety and depression in an effort to keep up. Many couples describe their relational dynamic as "two ships passing in the night" or "roommates" and that they are missing out on romantic and sexual connection.

Life for many people has become compartmentalized—boxed off into sections, without integration of the intimate connection that people say they desire.

If you create a narrative that intimate connection can only occur after 10 p.m. at night, of course you're going to feel disconnection. You're too tired. But what if you didn't box off your life into sections? Can you imagine integrating romantic, sensual, and tender behaviours into the daily minutiae of life?

As you go throughout your day, imagine a thread of intimacy weaving between you and your partner—even though you are not physically together. Think about your partner and make connection at least once a day in a romantic way. As you go about your daily living, integrate imaginative, creative and tender ways to connect with your partner while sharing a meal together, reading to your children, taking care of the house, or being with friends and family.

Consider:

~ *When you go grocery shopping, pick up a single flower for your partner*
~ *Put a jellybean or a chocolate on your partner's pillow before he goes to bed at night*

~ *Give each other a high-five when you have completed joint tasks such as getting the children to their activities on time, mowing the lawn, cleaning the house, or washing the windows*

~ *Send a "thinking of you" text*

~ *Reminisce about when you first met each other*

~ *Have a selection of cards on hand and every once in a while, tuck a card with a sweet note into your partner's handbag or briefcase before they leave for work*

~ *Express appreciation to your partner every day*

~ *End the day by telling each other what worked in your relationship for you today*

~ *Have a conversation about something interesting going on in the world*

~ *Change up the routine—you cook this time and the other will vacuum*

~ *Share household tasks, rather than divide them.*

21

CULTIVATE MINDFULNESS

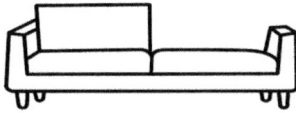

MINDFULNESS IS THE ACT OF PAYING ATTENTION, moment by moment, on purpose, and without judgment.

Mindfulness is an increasingly popular concept in the fields of medicine and psychology. It refers to an ongoing effort to be aware of your body and your mind, as well as your relationship to the environment around you. Mindfulness is not a state that you achieve, so much as it is an approach to life. Inherent to this concept is a commitment to yourself to become aware of what is occurring in your body, physiologically and emotionally. For example, by paying attention to your own physiological distress such as an elevated heart rate, clenched fists, furrowed brow, knots in stomach or shallow breathing, you will recognize when you feel anxious or angry.

What does mindfulness have to do with your relationship? Everything. By becoming aware, you can recognize when you are susceptible to reacting to your partner by lashing out in anger or by becoming defensive. The more aware you become, the better opportunity you have to take time to soothe yourself so you can respond to your partner in a way that fosters better communication. Most couples say they want better communication. You can start with mindfulness.

Some examples of physiological and psychological distress are:
- ~ Headaches
- ~ Stomachaches
- ~ Tight muscles
- ~ Sweating
- ~ Dizziness or lightheadedness
- ~ Trembling
- ~ Elevated heart rate
- ~ Fear
- ~ Disgust
- ~ Anger
- ~ Rage
- ~ Frustration
- ~ Worry
- ~ Confusion
- ~ Sadness.

Depending on the situation and the environment you find yourself in when experiencing emotional and physiological distress, you need to have several ways to calm your central nervous system.

If you are sitting at home or work:

~ Breathe—inhale and exhale through your mouth; exhale right down to your abdomen. The exhale is always available to you. The quality of your breathing is essential to overall health and wellbeing and is something to pay attention to throughout the day, all day long.

~ Feel whatever emotion you are experiencing, with acceptance and non-judgment. Resist saying, "I shouldn't feel that way."

~ Soften the muscles around your eyes, between your brows, jawline, cheeks and drop your shoulders.

~ Write your name with your buttocks when you're sitting in a chair. When you're upset you will tighten up in the pelvis and become a tight ass! This puts pressure on your stomach and diaphragm and causes you to breath more shallowly. When you write your name with your buttocks, you relax your pelvic floor and then organically start to breathe deeper. After you write your name, keep sitting quietly, close your eyes and listen to the sounds you hear.

~ Close your eyes and bring into your imagination a beautiful image of something that you find soothing—a landscape, beach, forest, sky, or mountains. (Do not put people in this image as they are potentially conflictual.)

If you are on the move:

~ Take a brisk walk or go for a run.

~ Jump.

~ Dance.

If you are at home:
- ~ Listen to comforting music.
- ~ Lay down, close your eyes, take a breath in and a long exhale out. Repeat the exercise ten times.
- ~ Light a tea light, set a timer for five minutes and stay focused on the flame.
- ~ Have a bath. Darken the room and light a few candles. Ignore phones, books, magazines, and other distractions. Lay back, close your eyes, and follow your breath.

If you are sitting in a car:
- ~ If you are in traffic, be mindful of the taillights around you. Notice where they're placed on the vehicle, the shape of them, are they LED or do they have bulbs? (The car manufacturing companies have decided to help us out with this endeavour by creating a whole variety of taillights. We're sure they did this to help you with your road rage!)

What strategies do I already use to soothe myself?
Are they as effective as I want them to be?
What other strategies do I think will be beneficial to me, given the particular environment I find myself in?

22

DETERMINE YOUR RESPONSE TO AN AFFAIR

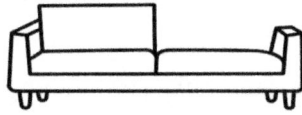

AN EXTRA-RELATIONAL AFFAIR (ERA) occurs when one person breaches an implicit or explicit agreement of sexual monogamy. Emotional affairs are also included in this category. Emotional affairs progress from a friendship with a person other than your partner to a greater level of personal intimacy and attachment. Hallmarks of an emotional affair are disclosing personal information of an intimate nature and turning to someone other than your partner during times of need or vulnerability.

We recommend that instead of promising not to have an affair, you fundamentally agree to share your vulnerability to having an affair ahead of *actually* engaging in an affair.

There are open relationships where couples agree to be committed to each other and *also* agree to have sexual and/or emotional relationships with other people. We advise, in this case, to discuss, and get clear as to the "rules" of your open relationship. Even in open relationships, an agreement can be breached if one partner chooses to break the agreement of the boundaries mutually set by the couple.

Both men and women engage in extra-relational affairs with equal fervor.

The following are comments we often hear when a person finds out about their partner's affair:

~ You hear about this happening in other people's relationships, but I can't believe this happened in ours.
~ She is the nicest person. I can't believe she would have done this.
~ I don't know who she is anymore. This is so unlike her.
~ And with my best friend too!
~ I said that an affair would be a deal breaker, but it's not.
~ How do I continue living with him knowing what he did?
~ I hate him and I love him.
~ How did I not see this coming?
~ I suspected so, but I didn't want to believe it.

Affairs create a crisis. If the couple stays together, the relationship will never be the same again. In some ways, this is good news. In other ways, this is the bad news. The good news is that the crisis most often stimulates personal and relational growth that benefits both people. The bad news is that affairs cast a shadow over the relationship that will always exist, hovering quietly in the background.

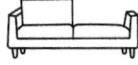

How vulnerable am I to an affair today? (From time to time, check in with yourself using this question.)

23

EXPRESS GENUINE PRIDE IN YOUR RELATIONSHIP

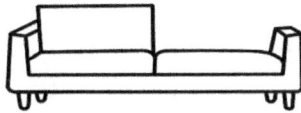

WE ARE ALL WELL AWARE THAT WOMEN AND MEN get together with friends and family and complain about their partners. There is a fine line, however, between getting support and advice from those in your close circle and complaining about your partner and your relationship.

When we see and hear people speak well of their partner at social events, work, family functions—even in therapy—a sense of pride exudes. This casts a warm glow over the relationship. We encourage people to be mindful of this and when you are out and about in your social circles and workplaces, practice speaking well of your partner. When your partner is with you, they will feel your love and your connection will be stronger.

Be consistent with expressing pride in your relationship when you are alone with your partner and when you are with others.

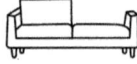

Make a mental note next time you are with your partner, whether alone or with others, to say something like, "We have some challenges, but mostly we are great together" or "I am really proud of what we have created together."

24

GO TO BED ANGRY

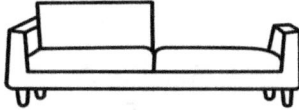

"DON'T GO TO BED ANGRY" is perhaps the most common and least helpful piece of advice given to young couples. People who try to follow this piece of social wisdom are more likely to quit from exhaustion than they are from having resolved a conflict.

Conflict is inescapable in any relationship. If you wish to optimize your odds for a successful outcome, you can start by creating a process regarding conflict resolution. If you are going to attempt a difficult conversation, whether it is about something you want, or about your hurt feelings, you want to be as resourced as possible:

~ Don't fight when you or your partner are tired. Save it for tomorrow.

~ Don't fight when you are hungry or have been drinking.

~ Don't fight for more than five minutes without a break You have already said everything. You are just repeating, only more loudly and insistently.

You regain perspective when you allow some distance and reflection in a conflict.

Following these guidelines requires that you are willing to be responsible for, and able to calm your own body, which is an essential skill in creating a successful relationship.

If you end the argument before the issue has been resolved, commit to following through with your partner at a specific date. That could be the next day or in a couple of days.

25

HAVE FUN

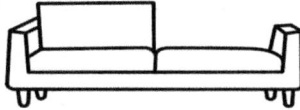

NEVER UNDERESTIMATE the importance of having fun. When first dating, fun is typically high on the agenda for the dating couple. However, somewhere over the course of a relationship, fun can become more elusive, with little attention being paid to this very important element. Couples tend to get "serious" about the business of their relationship, home, and hearth. Domestic tasks need to be accomplished, bills have to be paid, work issues need to be resolved, children need to be raised (if children are involved), groceries need to be bought—and conversations about all of these need to happen.

Make fun a top priority! Always. Build it in to your relationship. Plan for it. Make it as important as everything else that goes on your "to do" list. Don't compromise this part of your relationship.

It is each person's responsibility to make sure they are contributing not only to having ideas about what to do, but also to making sure the ideas are executed. Keep dating your partner throughout the course of your relationship.

If you are in a relationship, talk to your partner about the idea of building fun into your relationship daily. Let each other know what you consider to be fun and make a conscious decision to have fun every day.

26

LEARN FROM BETRAYAL

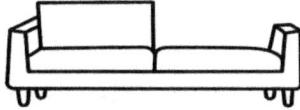

THE RESULT OF BETRAYAL IS THE LOSS OF INNOCENCE. We all enter a relationship with the expectation that we can put our faith in, and completely trust, our partner to be faithful. This is especially true when there has been an actual agreement on each person's part to be sexually faithful to each other.

While we often think of betrayal in the sexual context, there are all kinds of betrayals. A betrayal of some sort is inevitable in a relationship. Be it an emotional affair, a sexual affair, a withholding of information, financial secrets, a lie or neglect—we all have to deal with being betrayed and with the inevitable pain.

Losing innocence means you can no longer trust that you are safe from the struggles that plague other relationships. You now have to live in a world that has lost its security and you cannot always trust that your partner has your best interests at heart. The benefit of this loss is the gaining of wisdom. Your relationship, and the world, is not as secure as you thought it was and you now must become more self-reliant.

Adam was married to Julie for eighteen years. Although they had gone through some difficult times, he always assumed his relationship was solid. Then Julie had an affair. When the affair came to light, Adam was devastated. Adam insisted that Julie re-establish his trust. He was constantly questioning her and scanning for signs of betrayal. He wanted to regain his belief that she wouldn't betray him again. He demanded that Julie be responsible for his regaining trust by proving to him she would not betray him again.

Barbara suggested to Adam that he could no longer trust Julie, nor did he need to. Adam was confused by this and asked how he could possibly continue a relationship with Julie if he did not trust her. Barbara asked Adam if he believed Julie when she said she regrets having an affair and wants to stay married to him. Adam said that he did, but how was he to know that she wouldn't cheat again? Barbara went on to say that it's not possible for Adam to know for certain, nor does he need to. Adam was confused by this statement. Barbara told Adam that he now knows his relationship with Julie is not immune to betrayal and by staying in this relationship, he is taking a risk.

Barbara also insisted that if Adam chose to stay in the relationship, he must stop monitoring, grilling, and punishing Julie. Adam indicated he wanted to reconcile with Julie, however, he was stuck on the notion that he couldn't trust her. Barbara's advice to Adam was that while he couldn't trust Julie, and possibly would never again, who he needed to trust was himself.

"You need to trust that you will behave in a matter that is consistent with your own values and integrity and with the kind of marriage you want. You also need to trust yourself that you have what it takes to survive another betrayal, should one occur, by making decisions that are good for you. You can never have that same feeling of security you once had, but you can move forward in your relationship without any illusion of security. This will allow you to be more intentional in creating the kind of relationship you and Julie want."

It often takes a crisis in a relationship to jar a couple out of complacency or neglect. An affair is an undeniably painful way to have a couple sit up and take notice, but it catapults people into deciding about ending their relationship or creating something that is more satisfying to both of them.

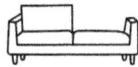

Discuss with your partner when and how you have felt betrayed. (These don't need to be big-ticket items; they may be of a less substantive nature.)

If you feel you are vulnerable to an affair, discuss with your partner.

27

LEARN TO LISTEN

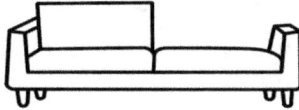

KNOWING HOW TO LISTEN FIRST IS A USEFUL TOOL for resolving conflict. The following is a suggested approach for actively listening to your partner to hear their point of view—a first step in resolving a conflict.

Note that the listener does not have to agree with the other's interpretation of events or the meaning that is ascribed to them. The job of the listener is to understand and to communicate that understanding to the speaker.

This can be illustrated by a conflict between Jack and Susi.

Susi's family has planned a get together on Saturday. The family is very close, and they are celebrating the return of Susi's brother who has been away for some time. Jack is up first and makes coffee, then begins to read the paper. Susi comes into the kitchen, pours a coffee, and asks Jack if he is going to get ready for the party. Jack replies that he is ready. He's showered and shaved and as this isn't a formal event, he believes the clothes he has on are fine. He continues to read the paper.

At two o'clock, Susie says, "We should go." Jack, in the meantime, has become involved in a novel and reluctantly agrees. He knows that sometime during the event he will have to use the washroom and so he brings his book along. They are the first to arrive and are greeted by Susi's mother and younger sister, Anne.

Anne, who is getting married later that year, says, "I've picked out the decorations for the head table. Do you want to see?"

Susi, of course, enthusiastically agrees. Jack, who does not care about wedding decorations, senses an opportunity to escape and retreats to the other room and resumes reading his book.

When the other family members arrive, Jack puts his book away and visits until dinner. He becomes aware that something is amiss when Susi picks a place at the table as far from him as possible. Following dessert, Jack, who is bored, asks his brother-in-law, Peter, if he is bored too. Peter, who lives near Jack and Susi, replies in the affirmative. Jack suggests that they both go to Peter's place and watch an action movie. Peter agrees. Jack goes up to Susi, gives her the car keys, tells her he and Peter are going to his place to watch a movie and he will walk home after.

When Jack gets home, Susi is already asleep in bed, squeezed into the four inches on the edge of her side, leaving a big icy patch in the middle of the bed. He arises before Susi in the morning and makes coffee, sits down, and continues reading his novel. Susi comes into the kitchen a little later. The look on Susi's face tells Jack that she is more than a little upset.

Susi: *I am really upset with you and I want to talk about it.*

Jack: *I know. There was a big icy spot in bed. Let me refresh my coffee and then I will listen.* (He returns from the kitchen, bringing a cup for Susi as well.) *OK, I can tell you are angry. Tell me what it's about.*

Susi: *I'm REALLY angry at you for being rude to my mother.* (Jack is confused as he has no memory of being rude to Susi's mother. Jack's commitment is to understand her experience, not to defend himself or explain his experience, at this point in the conversation.)

Jack: *I'm not sure what you're talking about. I don't remember being rude to your mother.*

Susi: *When we got to the house yesterday, you escaped as soon as you could and read your book instead of visiting with my family. When Mom came in and asked if you were bored, you said, "Oh, you have no idea", and returned to your book. Mom came back to the kitchen and had tears in her eyes because you hurt her feelings.* (Jack does not remember that exchange, but his job is still to communicate his understanding of Susi's experience, not to explain his own.)

Jack: *So, what you're angry about is that I was rude to your mother when she asked if I was bored.* (He was reflecting back both Susi's content and feelings.)

Susi: *Yes, and you got away from us as quickly as you could and then after dinner, you and Peter took off to watch a movie.* (This, Jack does remember!)

Jack: *If I'm understanding you correctly, you are mad because, not only was I rude to your Mother, but that I also escaped your company when Peter and I took off to watch a movie at his place. Is that correct?*

Susi: *Yes.* (Still visually upset.)

Jack: *I can tell you're still upset, so I think I'm missing something, and I want to get it.*

Susi: *And I was bored too, and you just left me.*

Jack: *Oh, so you felt abandoned by me yesterday, in addition to the other things?*

Susi (with a big sigh): *Yes, my feelings were hurt because I felt like you left me.*

In this vignette, Jack is still not convinced that he was rude. It does not, however, matter as he has achieved his goal of communicating to Susi that he understands, even if he doesn't agree with her perspective on the previous day.

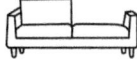

Next time your partner wants to share with you something important, keep in mind—first and foremost—to be in a listening role.

28

LISTEN TO IMPROVE COMMUNICATION

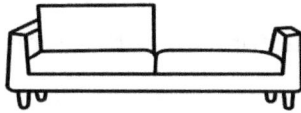

WITHOUT A DOUBT, the most common difficulty our clients want us to help them work through is a lack of communication in their relationship. We respond by asking them to talk about which aspect or aspects each is having difficulty with. The problem frequently boils down to an adversarial mindset. Couples approach disagreements as though they were barristers in a courtroom trying to "win" a conversation as opposed to partners trying to resolve conflicts in the most mutually beneficial manner. There are two major components of communication. One is listening with an attitude of curiosity and in a manner that invites the other to acknowledge thoughts, feelings, and experiences that may contradict your own. The second component is speaking honestly and courageously by revealing who you are—that is, expressing your thoughts, opinions, ideas, preferences, and feelings.

Conversations break down very quickly when the speaker adopts an obstinate or accusatory tone, such as: "This is the way things are and you just won't admit it!" This strategy never resolves a conflict.

Another common conversation breakdown occurs when an individual "mind reads". This is when the speaker, for example, insists they know what the other person is thinking—despite protests to the contrary. This exacerbates a conflict. Just like speaking in an accusatory tone, this strategy will often end a conversation.

Communication problems occur when one or both partners feel threatened by the differing thoughts and experiences of the other. People feel anxious when their partner expresses different opinions or has their own version of reality. The effort to bring the other person on side supersedes curiosity and acceptance of the other. Attempting to bring the other person over to your side will result in both people feeling frustrated, alienated, and not willing to disclose to each other.

The art of respectful communication is difficult to learn and to master. It involves letting go of the need to be right and the need to have your partner conform to your version of reality. Your partner has their own way of understanding the world, which may be frustrating to you at times.

*What differences do I see in my partner that create anxiety for me?
How does my partner experience anxiety as a result of our differences?*

29

MOVE BEYOND DECLARATION OF SELF

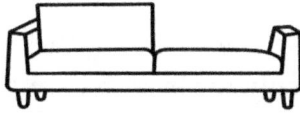

HERE'S A FUNNY THING ABOUT PEOPLE: we hate being categorized except when we love it. Who hasn't said something along the lines of, "I'm a Sagittarius, so I hate drama," or "I'm an INTP, so I love crossword puzzles"? Most people are only half-serious when they define themselves in these ways. However, it's not uncommon for one of our clients to adamantly declare, "This is just who I am". This statement is nearly always offered as an excuse to continue some undesirable behaviour.

"This is just who I am" is not a statement of fact. Rather, it is a declaration of an attachment to a narrow view of one's self. If you rigidly attach yourself to a specific personality characteristic, you deny the possibility of change, thereby letting yourself off the hook for whatever harm that characteristic might cause. You don't have to put in the work to change yourself because "that's just who you are". Neat trick.

But what if, instead, you said, "This is how I'm used to seeing myself" or "This is how I've experienced myself to date"? Now you have the space to evaluate whether a specific characteristic, behaviour, or belief is worth making the effort to change. Don't limit yourself with a declaration like, "My partner needs to accept that I'm just an impatient person". Instead, try, "I've experienced myself as an impatient person, which has caused problems between myself and my partner. I will learn to become more patient". Suddenly, the burden of responsibility has shifted, and a clear path to change has presented itself.

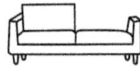

What characteristics have I expressed as "Just the way I am" or "That's how I was raised"?
What characteristics does my partner claim as intrinsic to who they are?

30

PREPARE FOR DIFFICULT CONVERSATIONS

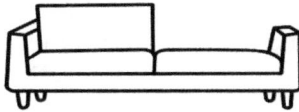

WE SEE COUPLES IN THERAPY when they lack the skills and maturity needed to have difficult conversations.

Some topics of difficult conversations are:
- ~ Sex
- ~ Money
- ~ Parenting styles
- ~ Resentments
- ~ Where to live
- ~ Option to have children
- ~ Relationships with friends and family
- ~ Jealousy, control, and power issues

~ Conflicting desires
~ Addictions
~ Betrayals

Here are some of the reasons people say they stop themselves from having difficult conversations:

~ It will hurt her.
~ He'll get mad.
~ She will give me the silent treatment.
~ She starts crying or leaves the house.
~ She pouts or becomes defensive.
~ He tells me I'm crazy.
~ He will put me down, dismiss me, or criticize what I am
~ saying.
~ We will end up arguing our points, without listening to each other's thoughts or feelings.
~ He will deflect responsibility or deny wrongdoing.
~ She will get defensive.
~ He'll say, "I can never please you."

Sometimes people enter into a conversation already having determined what their desired outcome is. This is problematic if their partner has a different desire. In difficult conversations, success is dependent on each person trying to understand the other's point of view.

Step One: Listen to what your partner has to say. Put your own agenda on the backburner while you *really* listen to what she is saying. Ask questions to learn more about what she is thinking and feeling. This is how you get to know her.

If you don't care about getting to know your partner and you just want what you want, then you won't be able have the kind of conversation you say you want.

Step One involves *both* people listening to each other's viewpoint.

Step Two: Once both of you feel that you have been heard, the conversation is finished. If your goal is to be heard and understood and you believe your partner has in fact done that, congratulations, you have success. If, however, your conversation involves a decision that needs to be made, move onto Step 3.

Step Three: Jim and Mary have $5000 to spend. Scenario A is that they both agree that they want to spend the money on a vacation. That's easy. Conversation done! Scenario B: Jim wants to put the money onto their mortgage. Mary wants to spend the money on a vacation. They both believe strongly in how this money should be spent. They have completed Step One by listening to each other's desires for how they want to spend the money. Each is heard and understood, but they still want what they want.

One option to resolve this disagreement is a compromise where $2,500 goes to the mortgage and $2,500 towards a vacation. However, a compromise is not always possible if one of the partners isn't interested in compromising or if a compromise is not feasible. (For example, in the case above, compromise would not be feasible if they could pay down the mortgage only in sums of $5,000 or more or if the vacation is more than $2,500.)

In this case, the couple arrives at what is known as a two-choice dilemma. This means one person won't get what they want and the other will.

It is important to determine what your attitude about losing will be. Will you be resentful about the decision or will you be graceful about it? We suggest you come to an agreement about that ahead of having the difficult conversation.

Practice active listening—hearing what your partner is saying. Ask questions for interest sake and get to know how your partner thinks and feels about the issue. Delay your own gratification of inserting your thoughts or opinions until later in the conversation.

31

PRIORITIZE EACH OTHER

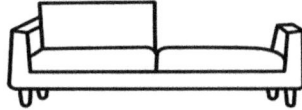

IF YOU WANT TO MAINTAIN CONNECTION, making your partner a top priority is crucial. What we often hear in therapy is that couples feel disconnected, describing themselves as roommates.

Our observation is that people don't want to miss out on anything. While we understand that individual pursuits, staying fit, hanging out with friends, and keeping up with social media are of interest to people—neglecting your partner will lead to disconnection.

If people want to maintain a healthy relationship, there will need to be a certain amount of sacrificing for the sake of the relationship. In order to maintain connection, your partner needs to know you will dedicate time and energy to them. This does not mean that you give everything up for your partner. In fact, your partner ought to come second in certain instances. What is important is that your partner gets the bulk of your time and presence.

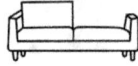

In what ways do I prioritize my partner?
In what ways do I fail to prioritize them?

32

RECIPROCATE

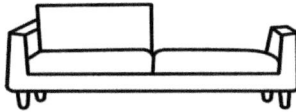

RECIPROCATING MEANS THAT EACH PERSON PUTS the needs of the other on par with their own. In every relationship, there are times when we do more than our share. For example, if your partner is under stress with work or family, you may do more than your share of the housework. When two people actively engage this way, it is rare that either one will complain that the other is neglectful. There is an underlying value of fairness and equality built into the foundation of the relationship.

If any person wants to have solely what they want in their life, without consideration of another, it is probably best not to be in a relationship. Part of a foundational premise of a healthy relationship is that you consider the needs and wants of the other.

What are the instances when I put my wants and needs ahead of my partner's and sacrificed their needs to get what I want?

What are instances when I felt my partner put my needs ahead of their own needs?

33

RELINQUISH MORAL HIGH GROUND

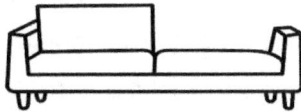

ONE OF THE SUREST WAYS TO DESTROY to destroy a relationship is to enter into a battle with your partner about who is the most right, the most hurt, the most moral, the best parent, the most honest, the most thoughtful, etc. This is a recipe for disaster.

Jeremy and Olivia are having financial troubles.

Olivia: *You have no discipline. You spend money as if it was water and if you keep this up, we will never get out of debt.*

Jeremy: *That's not fair, you just went out and bought a new pair of shoes last week and anyway I work longer hours than you do.*

Olivia: *Well I needed new shoes and you spend money on things we don't need and just get us further behind. You never think.*

Jeremy: *You're such a nag. I never get on your back about you going out for lunch.*

Olivia: *Well I certainly don't go out nearly as much as you do. Anyway, I'm more responsible than you are.*

Jeremy: *Well aren't you the best money manager in the city.*

Rather than trying to solve the issue, this couple seems more interested in who has the better position in the argument. Another righteous scenario looks like this:

Charlie: *I was really disgusted by you going out of your way to flirt with every Tom, Dick, and Harry at the party last night.*

Kelly: *I wasn't flirting. I was just being sociable.*

Charlie: *Yeah well, I would never be THAT SOCIABLE with other men, especially when I am with you. You were embarrassing. You have the morals of an alley cat.*

Kelly: *Well, you're not so perfect yourself you know. Last month you got drunk and made an ass of yourself.*

Charlie: *I still don't drink as much as you do, and I certainly don't come on to other men when I do.*

Kelly: *OOOH, I'm with Mr. Perfect.*

In both of these examples, the partners are more interested in their moral position than they are in fixing the issue. Whenever we claim moral high ground, we are avoiding responsibility and wanting our partner to carry the blame. While it may be true in the above example that Charlie would not behave as flirtatiously as Kelly in a social situation, he will certainly behave in other ways that Kelly would not.

If you are committed to creating a healthy relationship, you have to be willing to give up the fight for moral high ground.

Be mindful of any time you say, "I would never…", ask yourself if you are claiming moral high ground.

34

REPAIR AND LET GO

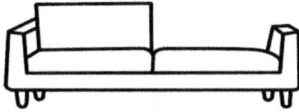

WE CANNOT OVERSTATE THE IMPORTANCE of doing repair work in your relationship. When you do something to harm another person, either through words or actions or through neglect, it is imperative to repair the harm done.

If your partner expresses to you that they are hurt by something you did or neglected to do—instead of denying it, be accountable and own up to what you did or didn't do. Even if you feel shame over your actions, confront your shame by holding yourself accountable—redemption is right around the corner. You can always redeem yourself by repairing and then being mindful of your harmful actions or neglectful behaviour. This will go a long way towards your partner respecting and liking you.

When repair is not done, lingering negative feelings occur, which will result in your partner disconnecting from you. This will be evident in your partner not wanting physical or sexual intimacy.

Examples of repair:

"I said some hurtful things to you. I want you to know that because of how I behaved, I know this resulted in you feeling confused, sad, lonely, alienated, angry, disillusioned, and disappointed."

"I forgot your birthday two years in a row. The story you likely make up about me is that I don't care about you or put you as a priority. I can understand why you don't want to get close to me. I will mark your birthday on my calendar a month in advance every year and plan something beautiful for you."

"I behaved badly when I threw a temper tantrum. I will be mindful of how my behaviour impacts you and I will stop to think before I say something. I will work hard to take care of my anger, so I don't project it on to you."

Once a repair has been initiated, it is up to your partner to accept the repair. Acceptance of the repair sounds like this: "I am glad to hear you acknowledge how your behaviour impacted on me, resulting in my not wanting to get close to you. I do appreciate you bringing attention to the things you mentioned, and I give you credit for the work you are doing to keep our relationship strong and healthy."

It's important to understand that once a repair is made, the person on the receiving end of the repair is in the power position. They will now determine where the relationship goes from here—by accepting or rejecting the repair.

Think of an issue you need to repair. How would you word it?

35

RE-WRITE THE MARITAL VOWS

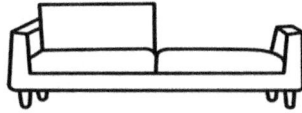

AFTER MANY YEARS of providing couples therapy, we have concluded that traditional marriage vows are insufficient. The standard ritual in North America has a couple promise a lifetime together "for better or for worse, for richer, for poorer, in sickness and in health, to love and to cherish, from this day forward, until death do us part."

Simple enough. So why do we have so much trouble keeping these vows? The problem isn't that people are incapable of committing to and sustaining long-term relationships. Rather, the idea of marriage, as exemplified by these vows, is fundamentally impractical.

Traditional vows imply nothing of the everyday stresses a marriage will face. Nor do they acknowledge the fact that individuals change.

The twenty-five-year-old who makes a lifelong commitment is a very different person, in very different circumstances, from the fifty-year-old who may struggle to honour it. The standard "'til death do us part" oath imagines love as something that can be frozen in time with the incantation, "I will."

Instead, we believe that couples should treat their vows as declarations of intent, while recognizing that a relationship is something that changes and grows along with the individuals that comprise it. With that in mind, we offer the following vows for consideration:

~ I promise to take care of myself, mentally and physically, in order to remain the kind of person who can best give and receive love.

~ I promise to consider your thoughts and feelings, even when they are different from my own. I promise to share my thoughts and feelings honestly, even if they might hurt you. However, I will never intentionally be cruel.

~ I promise to nurture my imagination and yours so our life together can be interesting, loving, and alive.

~ I will take care of my emotional self, my intellectual self, my physical self, and my spiritual self.

~ I will work toward creating a safe and sacred space between you and me where I am willing to be vulnerable with you. I will take care of you, and I will have your back.

~ I will recognize that we change, and I will accept that in myself and in you. I will have open and curious eyes to see you in new ways and through a fresh pair of eyes and an open heart.

~ I will be open to being aware of when I am rigid and inflexible and not open to what you have to say. I will recognize when I have a strong need to be right and how that shuts down communication.

~ I will be available to hear when I take you for granted. I will be grateful for who you are and what you bring into my life.

~ I will be open to your feedback when I don't recognize the things that I have committed to recognize.

~ Together with you, I commit to creating beauty in our home.

~ I will commit to nurturing my imagination so our life together can be interesting, alive, and have a strong heartbeat.

~ I will pause and think before I speak because doing so is a radical act of sanity and love. I will be honest with you in sharing my feelings and thoughts, and I will strive to do so in a respectful and non-violent way. I will be open to listening to your thoughts and feelings in a respectful way, even if they are different from mine or if what you are saying is hard to hear.

~ I will commit to compromise and negotiation.

~ I will commit to not running from difficult times. I will stay and do the hard work even though I may not know what or how to do it. I will be open to your influence. I will repair a connection when we become disconnected. I will say I am sorry and will own up to my own shortcomings instead of blaming you and withdrawing.

~ I will commit to my own growth and I will support you in yours.

Of these above "vows", which do I agree with? Disagree with? Find difficult to commit to?

36

SELF CONFRONT

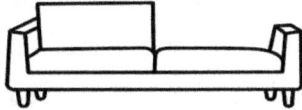

IMPLICIT IN ALL RELATIONSHIPS is that you *will* receive complaints and feedback from your partner. Ideally, you will receive many more compliments and statements of appreciation than complaints. Appreciative statements fuel the relationship in a healthy way. Complaints and feedback of a more critical nature have potential for individual and relational growth—should you be up for the challenge. When both people in a relationship are up for this challenge, you have an opportunity to create a vibrant and exciting adult relationship.

When you receive a complaint or a request for change from your partner, what is that experience like for you? What do you feel? Think? How does your body react? If you are not currently in a romantic relationship, what is your experience when you receive a complaint or a request for change from a friend, a family member, or a colleague?

Most often, people immediately become defensive. We have a built-in survival system and when we feel threatened, whether that be emotionally or physically, our survival mechanism, better known as the fight or flight response, kicks into gear.

For example, Tina says to Derek, "I seem to be the one who does all of the organizing of our social calendar. I enjoy doing this, but it would be really nice if you would plan something once in a while." If this comment is interpreted as a criticism by Derek, he will likely make a defensive response such as, "I can never do anything right by you."

Confronting yourself when you are aware that you feel threatened is a mindful act. When you start to feel your jaw clench, your stomach turn, or your hands tighten, this is your first clue that your body is getting primed for fight or flight. To self-confront is to be mindful and take accountability for what is happening to you both physiologically and emotionally. If you don't do this, you are likely to react in a knee-jerk way, activating the fight or flight—neither response being helpful to your relationship.

Our survival mechanisms are engaged in order to "protect thyself" first, giving zero consideration to the relationship in that moment. This is the time when harm is usually done in the relationship. You can avoid this harm if you self-confront. You can ask yourself the questions: "What am I experiencing in my body right now?" and "What am I feeling right now?"

This process allows for a personal inquiry into your own experience, so that you can then engage the higher functioning part of your brain to figure out how you want to respond to your partner.

The opposite of this is being unaware of what is happening for you and reacting to your partner in a defensive, angry, and hostile manner. This results in wounds that need to be repaired. While repair is necessary, if a pattern of negative response-repair continues for a long period of time, couples start to feel alienated and disconnected from each other.

A further step in self-confrontation is inquiring into what stories you are telling yourself about your partner. Let's go back to the example above where Derek is asked by his partner to plan some social engagements. The story Derek wrote in his head was, "I can never do anything right according to Tina." If he were to self-confront, he would be aware that his jaw may be clenching, and he was feeling frustrated. He would then inquire into what is causing the frustration and recognize that he was writing the story that his partner thinks he never does anything right. In this self-confrontation process, Derek could ask himself if that story is actually true. Here's the kicker—even if Derek thinks it might be true, he could still choose to simply respond to the request, "It sounds like it's important to you that I step up and plan some of the social activities. That would mean a lot to you and perhaps take some of the pressure off of you."

Self-confrontation means holding the mirror up to yourself first—prior to blaming your partner or becoming defensive in your relationship. If you don't do this, it is guaranteed that you and your partner will have plenty of difficulty. If you are interested in minimizing conflicts, become aware of your interactions every day. What are your emotions? What is happening in your body? Pay attention to the stories you are creating in your mind.

In some instances, people self-confront too well and to such an extent that they take on more accountability than is theirs. For these people, we advise that you make yourself aware of what is your work and what is your partner's. You do neither yourself nor your partner a service by doing work that's not yours to do.

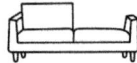

How did I react the last time my partner or someone else provided me with constructive feedback?

37

STOP TAKING IT PERSONALLY

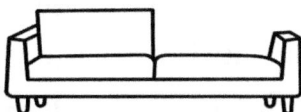

LIFE BECOMES IMMEASURABLY EASIER once we realize that our partner's behaviour, especially the behaviour we deem offensive, is not about us. Accepting this is one of the most difficult challenges we face as adults. This doesn't mean that we aren't impacted when our partner says or does something harmful— but their behaviour says more about them than it does about us. What *is* about us is our own response to another's behaviour.

If, for example, your partner tells you that you are "self-centered, only thinking of yourself all the time," you may feel offended and take their statement personally. If you can stop yourself from instantly feeling offended, you can examine whether your friend's assertion is accurate or not. If you determine it is not true, then there's really no reason to be offended as that is about their perception and not about you. If it is accurate, then you can take that opportunity to decide if you want to make a change or not.

We are all born with the narcissistic sense that the world revolves around us. Babies experience their world and their experience as all that there is. As children age, they become aware that their worlds are different from those of others.

By the time people reach their early teens, they have no doubt that they are different from others, especially their parents and other adults. Despite this awareness, teenagers are also absolutely convinced that their reality is the only one. Teenagers are aware that other people's behaviour has an impact on them, but they are, by and large, not aware of the impact they have on others. They experience themselves as subjects but are not yet able to observe themselves as objects.

As we move into our twenties, our developmental task is to become aware of the impact that our behaviour has on those around us. Our sense of who we are is still dependent on the feedback we receive. This is a reflected sense of self, meaning, "I know I'm lovable if you say you love me."

It is in the next stage of maturity, however, that it becomes possible to understand that other's negative communication to us is not personal.

People start to become aware that their interpretation of someone's behaviour will determine their response more than the behaviour itself. This realization brings a sense of freedom, as we no longer take personally what other people think or do. It is not personal. Often, one has to be middle-aged before this awareness is possible.

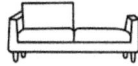

When have I reacted to someone and taken their behaviour personally?

38

TAKE A VACATION
TO RECONNECT

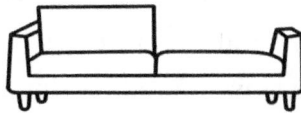

THE UNDERLYING ASSUMPTION in this chapter heading is that the couple has in fact disconnected from each other. This is a correct assumption as most couples cite a lack of connection as a primary reason for attending couples' therapy.

With respect to taking a vacation together in order to reconnect, we offer the following:

First, don't place too many expectations that any given vacation will be the only answer to the problem of disconnection. It can, though, be an important time to spend alone together to focus solely on each other, having no other day-to-day distractions.

Prior to leaving on vacation, discuss what is important to you while being away on your vacation. For example, is it important to do things together that you love? If so, research your vacation location to see what is available and make time for activities you enjoy.

Is it important for you to reconnect sexually? If so, plan to be intentional about restoring sexual intimacy and take along some massage oils, candles, clothing and lingerie that will set the mood.

If it's important for you to spend some time together while on vacation discussing how to keep the connection alive in your daily life, then make time for that. Articulate what is important to you to keep the connection alive. Have a strategy for maintaining connection once back in your daily routine. Keep it positive while on vacation.

Talk about when you first met, what you loved about each other. Sometimes people focus on the negatives about their partner— make time to remember what attracted you to each other.

If each person in the relationship acknowledges that they have been neglectful of nurturing the relationship, then it's time to re-commit to each other your intention of engaging in the relationship in a manner that supports growth, fun, and connection.

Let go of the "roles" you have in your daily life—husband, wife, partner, mother, father, worker, friend, sibling, child, co-worker—

and bring in the playful part of you—the adventurer, the lover, the free spirit.

Eat great food, drink great beverages, dance, laugh, and be playful. A vacation isn't a great time to focus on attempting to resolve relationship issues—that is best saved for work in couples' therapy.

Plan a vacation together. Using the above ideas, discuss what is important to you for your upcoming vacation.

39

THINK BEFORE YOU SPEAK

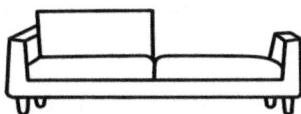

BEING INTENTIONAL MEANS TRAINING YOURSELF to think before you speak. Taking a moment to consider your words, rather than letting them spill out unfiltered, allows you to regulate your impact on those around you. Not only does this minimize the emotional stress—and hurt you might cause your friends and loved ones—it helps you become the kind of person that others want to be around.

Kelly grew up in a family where negativity was the default mode. Her father had a temper and her mother processed the world by pointing out everything wrong with it. She regularly projected her pessimism onto other people, ascribing negative intentions onto innocent behaviours. As a result, Kelly was defensive, quick to anger, and exhausting to be around.

At one point in Kelly's young adulthood, a close friend confronted her about her pessimistic attitude. She told Kelly that if she didn't change this outlook, she could look forward to an unhappy and lonely life. Kelly was gobsmacked, not just at the prospect of losing a relationship, but at the realization of how profoundly her negativity impacted those around her.

From that point, Kelly made a concerted effort to retrain her attitude. She chose to focus on what she liked in people rather than what she disliked. Kelly decided to interact with the world by appreciating the things she enjoyed in it. Of course, she was not impervious to irritation and stress. She still got defensive and angry from time to time, but she trained herself to process these emotions before she vocalized or acted on them. While she's not perfect in catching herself before reacting negatively, she is proud of the changes she made in her outlook on her life and the positive impact this intentionality has had on her relationships.

Do I have a habit of reacting instead of reflecting?
Have I had a relationship with a partner who reacted before reflecting? How did I feel?

40

THINK OUTSIDE THE BOX

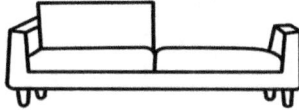

ALL KINDS OF CREATIVE PROBLEM SOLVING occurs in the therapy room regarding how a person can be personally fulfilled in a mutually satisfying relationship.

We encounter many people that, while they love their partner and want to be with them, they also love their autonomy. They want to live in a separate home, while maintaining a relationship with their partner. We regularly hear, "I want to have my own space where I am free to do what I want in my own time. I still want to be in a relationship with a partner, but just live in a different home."

This desire for autonomy reflects the central premise of *fully half committed*—people declare they are happier, living on their own, while still being in a relationship. We work with couples who are actively working on creative living arrangements of various kinds. Depending on whether there are children involved in blended family situations or whether people have no children, it isn't unusual for people to contemplate non-traditional ways of living. We encourage the exploration of various possibilities.

What intriguing ideas, if any, you have thought of regarding non-traditional living arrangements?

41

UNDERSTAND LOW SEXUAL DESIRE

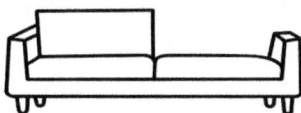

A COMMON COMPLAINT we hear from clients is that one or the other has low sexual desire. The most common reasons for this lack of passion are:

Busy with the responsibilities of life
Many people believe that sex should be spontaneous. But when couples are busy, spontaneity doesn't always appear. Make sexual intimacy a priority. Think less about how to feel desire. Just do it— as once you engage in sex, you may find that you become aroused.

Too much time together
Too much closeness often results in a loss of mystery about your partner. This can diminish sexual desire. Desire thrives in mystery

and newness. Consider spending a day apart from one another without disclosing what you're going to do. When you meet up with your partner again, share your adventure.

A lack of imagination

Make an effort and then keep making it. Bringing imagination and ideas into your sexual relationship stimulates sexual desire. It also goes a long way in preventing boredom and passivity from sneaking into your relationship. Here's some ideas: Consider reading erotica together, or visiting your local love shop together. Tap into your senses of touch, sight, sound, smell, and taste to explore what turns you on and then role play or plan a sex-filled weekend away.

Excessive use of pornography

Excessive use of pornography can interfere with a person's ability to connect physically and emotionally with their partner. This often leaves the other partner feeling neglected, which in turn leads to resentment.

Poor hygiene

This one really should be a no-brainer, but it's an issue that comes up more often than you might expect. It's difficult to get turned on for someone who regularly smells bad.

Anger or resentment

Prolonged resentment leads to withdrawal, withholding, and stonewalling. If you want to have sex, work on repairing outstanding issues first.

Body image issues

If you are critical of your body or your partner's, you likely won't want to have sex. You can either address the issue (by being active, exercising, eating well, and taking care of yourself), or accept your body the way it is. Or, better yet—do both.

Not thinking about sex

When we ask people how often during the day they think about sex, answers vary. For those people who have low to no sexual desire, the answer is often "not at all". If you're not even getting your mind involved in thinking about sex, it's difficult to get your body connected to the idea. Go ahead, think about your erotic self. Think about sensual pleasure. Think about looking and feeling sexy.

Lack of like, love, or respect for your partner

This problem is obviously bigger than sex. It's occasionally possible to re-kindle love, but if there's no respect, you should think long and hard about whether this is a relationship you want to, or ought to, be in.

Fear of sharing kinks

Risking rejection from someone who is important to you requires a great deal of courage. Sharing your wants and desires means that you may experience shame. This is part of the human condition. You will have to decide whether you want to take this risk. The potential problem with not disclosing to your partner is that you will be keeping your sexual proclivities private. When someone chooses not to disclose to their partner, they often find a way to fulfill their desires, often resulting in a betrayal.

Depression

Depression interferes with every aspect of life. It stifles a person's sex drive and makes them far less appealing to their partner. There's no easy solution for this problem, but it can be overcome, usually with a combination of medication and therapy. Seek treatment as soon as you can.

Grief and loss

Be patient. Grief can interfere with sexual desire, but it's usually temporary. If you get stuck in the loss, however, consider therapy and other external support.

Asexual partner

You may have a partner who is not interested in sex at all and never has been. It is best to consult with a therapist.

Lack of sexual chemistry

This is more common than people want to admit! Whether the sexual chemistry that existed at the time of courting has eroded or the sexual chemistry never existed between partners, as lack of sexual chemistry is problematic.

When you don't experience sexual desire for your partner and none of the above seem to be what you are experiencing, then do not focus on trying to force a feeling of desire for your partner. Instead, engage in the seduction, romance and sexual intimacy and see where that takes you. You may discover that desire shows up after you get aroused. Being sexually intimate will potentially make you want to have sex more often.

Have a conversation with your partner regarding the frequency and the type of sexual connection each of you would like. What is not enough, too much, and just right? Make this an on-going conversation throughout the course of your relationship as sexual preferences change over time.

42

UNDERSTAND SHAME

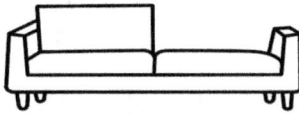

FEELING SHAME is a universal mammalian experience (unless you're a psychopath or a cat). It is an emotional response to being seen, or perceived to being seen, in a negative light. It is a powerful and effective tool to motivate us towards social compliance. One does not get to choose if they experience shame or not. It is an auto-response occurring sub-cortically in the limbic brain.

We all make mistakes, behave badly, are neglectful, and cause hurt to our relationships. Shame is a healthy consequence to these behaviours. Shame is only of concern if redemption does not take place. Redemption is a result of relationship repair. Repair is an essential part of a healthy relationship and occurs when re-connection is offered—and more importantly—allowed.

When repair is not offered and redemption does not take place, a chronic sense of humiliation may occur.

We may invite others into shame without being aware of it. Meet Luis and Will. Luis gets up most mornings before Will and makes coffee. He also goes to work before Will. Will usually joins Luis for coffee to spend some time with his partner before he leaves for work.

Luis watches Will come into the kitchen. Possibly to be humorous, he says, "So you decided to get up, did you?"

Will, drops his head, experiencing a shame response and feeling dejected. He responds, "Yeah, I wanted to spend some time with you."

Even though there was no intent on Luis's part to shame, dejection is Will's emotional experience and therefore repair is necessary. Healthy repair in this instance requires that the couple be aware of the shame and make an effort to reconnect.

Contrast this with Luis seeing Will enter the kitchen, "Good morning love, I'm glad you've come to join me."

Will's head comes up and he smiles.

Be mindful of any tendency you may have to shame your partner. Invite discussion with your partner about when you or they feel shame.

43

UNCOVER AND ACKNOWLEDGE
YOUR HIDDEN TERMS

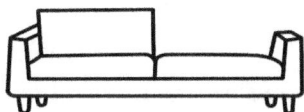

HAND IN HAND, Andrea and Theo stand before friends and family and pledge to love, honor and cherish one another. Though many others have made the exact same promise, rarely have expressions of love been uttered with such sincerity. No one in attendance can doubt Andrea's and Theo's devotion to the other. The guests erupt in cheers and tears when the officiant pronounces them married.

Not all commitments are officiated by clergy or presided over by witnesses. Often times, commitments are not declared in a single event, but are manifested over time through acts of mutual affection, generosity, and self-sacrifice. Beneath the surface, where the couple's best selves exchange good faith promises of love and devotion … there is a *basement*. In this basement, there is a second ceremony taking place, where the couple's insecure and wounded parts are cutting another deal with terms so hidden that neither party is fully conscious of their own condition.

Andrea and Theo are an imaginary couple, but their basement ceremony is typical:

Andrea: *I'm the oldest of five children. I was the princess until my parents started having more kids. I eventually became the babysitter for my younger siblings. When my dad got sick, I had to look after him too. I never forgave him for that. I felt abandoned. I want to be your princess and I expect you to attend to my every need and desire. If you don't do this, I will resent you and my eye will always be looking for something better. Do you accept these terms? Yes, you do!*

Theo: *My mother didn't want me when I was born, but felt she had no choice. She told me in lots of little ways. She may have loved me, but she treated me as a reminder of everything she had to give up in order to satisfy the expectations of her community. Your job now is to supply me with never-ending love and acceptance. You can never criticize me, no matter how much I deserve it. If you do, it will hurt my feelings and I will punish you for that. Most importantly, you will always be available for sex because that is how I know that I am cared for. Do you accept these terms? Yes, you do!*

Is the marriage of Andrea and Theo doomed to fail? It's difficult to say. Their commitment to each other is genuine, but their unacknowledged terms are incompatible with each other's. In fact, these hidden terms are incompatible with any truly successful relationship, since the terms are completely self-oriented and relationships demand a high degree of sacrifice. Moreover, Andrea and Theo have made themselves reliant on the other for validation and a sense of wellbeing, which means any normal amount of conflict they encounter will be amplified and re-amplified on both sides. With sustained effort, Andrea and Theo could keep their insecurities in check, but unfortunately, neither has acknowledged their hidden terms even to themselves. Moreover, these terms lay in their unconscious mind. What can be certain is that Andrea and Theo can look forward to a future filled with resentment and recriminations. That is, of course, unless they make the effort to drag their wounded and insecure parts up from the basement.

Our hidden selves will never totally disappear, but when brought into the light, their ability to inflict harm is drastically reduced. Therapy can be useful in this process because practitioners are trained to assist people in bringing the unconscious into consciousness.

Even without professional therapy, it is possible to confront your wounds and hidden terms if you are honest with yourself. Keep in mind that we have blind spots that prevent us from seeing parts of ourselves that need to be brought into awareness.

Write down what you think is your secret deal. Write down what you think your partner's secret deal might be.

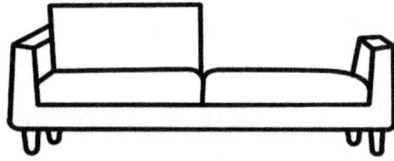

CONCLUSION

At the beginning of your relationship, you and your partner will not know the challenges ahead. Many couples in new relationships believe they will be the unique ones who will have ongoing harmony. They are wrong. You will experience situations that you will not be able to easily figure out. Some of these experiences may be jealousy, insecurity, psychological health issues, sexual problems, financial challenges, career changes, parenting challenges, and family-of-origin issues.

You may even reach a point where one of you may feel "out-of-love" and will choose to end the relationship—but most problems that you experience are solvable if you seek help before it's too late.

You are not supposed to know how to handle everything. This does not mean you are a failure. This means you are right where you are supposed to be in terms of personal and relational development. This is good news. It is an opportunity to learn new skills, to heal from past wounds, and to collaborate with your partner to grow together.

You will be able to solve some of these challenges together without difficulty and other challenges you won't. Seek professional assistance when you are struggling, especially if the difficulties are causing a rift. Do not wait. Like a bad tooth, the longer you leave treatment, the more decay. The longer an emotional and/or sexual rift goes on, the more difficult it is to repair.

You bring more than your individual self to the relationship. You bring your personal history, relationships with your family and friends, worldview, political view, biases, judgments, perceptions, and preferences. You will not be "on the same page" of every issue and decision as your partner. Couples love to say they want to be on the same page—but let us repeat—you will not be. Negotiation skills and compromise are needed in these situations.

The days of 30-year, 40-year and 50-year marriages are a thing of the past. People are no longer staying in relationships "til death do us part". Personal happiness has taken precedent over relationship longevity. For those people attempting to maintain their relationship and be personally happy, creating a conscious and intentional relationship is imperative to a vibrant and happy relationship.

Meaningful endurance is required to work together through relationship struggles. You will experience unhappiness, confusion, fatigue, ambivalence, frustration, anger, sadness, and loneliness in your relationship. You will also experience happiness, joy, peace of mind, bliss, contentment, and excitement. The temptations of being fully half committed will make an appearance at different times throughout your relationship. Inherent in relationships is the fact that you re-choose your partner many times over the course of a relationship. You decide!

BIOGRAPHIES OF
THE AUTHORS

BARBARA MORRISON

Barbara Morrison lives in the beautiful Canadian prairies, in Saskatoon, Saskatchewan and has been in private practice since 2003. Prior to beginning her private practice, Barbara worked in family counselling clinics in Saskatoon, Saskatchewan and Calgary, Alberta. Barbara offers individual, couples and family therapy. For two decades, she has facilitated workshops and presented at speaking engagements.

In 1986, Barbara graduated with a degree in Social Work from the University of Regina. In 2003, she graduated with her Master's degree in Clinical Social Work from the University of Calgary, with a specialty in couples therapy.

Barbara has two decades of professional development training in many therapeutic modalities. Pertinent to this book on romantic relationships, she has worked with the best of the best in couples training; David Schnarch, Ellyn Bader, Peter Pearson, Terry Real, Esther Perel, Harville Hendrix, and Sue Johnson.

Along with Barbara's focus on couples' therapy, she also specializes in the area of anxiety disorders. Coincidentally, these two areas dovetail from beginning to end throughout the therapy process.

ED RISLING

Ed Risling was born in Wilkie, Saskatchewan and has been in private practice in Saskatoon, Saskatchewan, Canada since 1985. Prior to starting his private practice, Ed worked in northern British Columbia as the head of an Inpatient Unit. In Saskatoon, Ed worked in Child and Youth Psychiatry at University Hospital. Prior to his time in northern BC and his current field of work, Ed sold bibles door to door in Arkansas in 1970.

Ed graduated in 1974 with a diploma in Psychiatric Nursing from Wascana Institute in Saskatchewan and with a degree in Social Work from the University of Regina in 1990.

He has trained in Hynotherapy with Maggie Phillips, an accomplished hypnotherapist from University of California–Berkley. Ed's further training includes working with Redecision

Therapy (Western Institute for Group and Family Therapy, Watsonville, California) and Self-Regulation Therapy (Centre Foundation for Trauma Research and Education – Kelowna, B.C.).

HOW TO FIND US

Barbara Morrison, BSW, MSW, RSW
www.saskatoonrelationshipclinic.ca
www.broadwaytherapy.ca
Saskatoon, Saskatchewan
Canada

Ed Risling, RPN, BSW, RSW
www.saskatoonrelationshipclinic.ca
www.prairietherapists.com
Saskatoon, Saskatchewan
Canada

www.ingramcontent.com/pod-product-compliance
Lightning Source LLC
LaVergne TN
LVHW051236080426
835513LV00016B/1625